C000003430

The
Fortean Times
Book of the
Millennium

Kevin McClure

About the author

Kevin McClure writes the Millennium Watch column for *Fortean Times*. He has researched extraordinary beliefs and events for more than 25 years and has investigated religious visions, alien abductions, strange lights, angels, demons, and all kinds of paranormal phenomena.

First published in Great Britain in September 1996 by John Brown Publishing Ltd, The Boathouse, Crabtree Lane, Fulham, London SW6 6LU, UK.

Tel 0171 470 2400. Fax 0171 381 3930.

ISBN 1-870870-786

Printed and bound in Great Britain
by Staples Printers of Rochester

The
Fortean Times
Book of the
Millennium

Kevin McClure

Contents

PERSONAL ENCOUNTERS
....

I think it was early in 1973 that Jesus Christ booked in. I was working in a large hostel for homeless men in south-east London, interviewing the new arrivals on shift-work. It was after midnight, it had been snowing heavily, and it was darned cold out. This young man was lightly dressed, mostly in white, in sandals without socks.

He was very distant to start with, but after his obligatory shower and being checked for lice, he came through for interview. He was quite sure that he was Jesus Christ, and that he had a mission to fulfil. Because I needed it to fill in the appropriate forms to give him a bed for the night in a dormitory in this barely-converted workhouse, he told me the name he had been born with, and given the circumstances we had a fair conversation. After a while he was clearly tired, and I had work to do. We had some soup we could heat up for late arrivals, and he seemed pleased when I said I'd bring him some.

When I came back downstairs with his food a few minutes later, he was leaving, going back out into the snow still inadequately dressed, cold and unfed. I asked him why he was leaving and he said something to the effect that he had to. I asked him whether he'd just stay to have the soup, and he said that he'd do without. He explained that he was Jesus Christ, and I understood him to mean that Jesus Christ would, by his nature, go without. I didn't see him again.

It wasn't the first time I'd encountered the fringes of belief. In 1968, just after I left school, I visited the Spiritualist Church in Woodford, in East London. This was the first Spiritualist service I'd been to, and although I was given a warm welcome from a lively group, the service was uneventful for me. I didn't receive a message from the visiting medium, and I was really quite grateful for that. Afterwards, over tea and biscuits, I listened to conversations. A lady of or so was telling how she'd seen a vision of "Jesus Christ in a hedge". Those were her exact words. Neither she nor the others seemed too amazed, but neither was there any apparent disbelief. I'd met my first visionary.

Then, I was a fairly committed Christian, considering career choices of Church of England vicar or clinical psychologist, depending on how university turned out. Looking back, I think that some of the excitement of Christianity was that it asserted the reality of an existence beyond ours, and the prospect of being a priest would offer me a special place in the interface between those existences. The clinical psychologist idea probably had some of the same elements, too. I've always been interested in the outer limits of belief and conviction, which was why I'd chosen to be in that church.

Over the few months before university, I became quite involved in Spiritualism, and I learned a lot about experiences that are visible and audible to some, but invisible and inaudible to me and almost everybody else. I joined the Spiritualist Association of Great Britain, where bigger and better experiences and experiencers could be found. I went to meetings at the College of Psychic Science, with similar results.

I helped revive the university Society for Psychical Research. While I worked towards a degree in theology, we invited channellers, mediums, witches, psychic researchers, flying saucer buffs and other fascinating characters to present their beliefs and demonstrate their abilities. And when, eventually, university and theology and I parted company, I ended up working at the hostel for homeless men.

The Jesus Christ I met there wasn't the same Jesus Christ that the woman at the Spiritualist church had seen in the hedge. It wasn't the same one that I'd believed in when I was going to become a priest. There are so many different Jesus Christs for so many people, just as there are different Virgins and Mothers of Christ, and angels, and aliens, and demons, and who knows what else. They all deserve the respect and consideration that I hope I managed to give to that man in the snow in Peckham, but it isn't possible to believe in them all, or to all live our lives as they would all wish us to.

In bringing together this extraordinary collection of prophecy, prediction, strange information and experience, I'm not asking you to believe in anything at all. I've tried to provide the facts, and some understanding of how they've come about: what you make of them is up to you. All I ask is that you treat anybody's beliefs with respect – more and stranger than these will no doubt be coming soon.

Kevin McClure
July 1996

Chapter 1

WAITING FOR THE END OF THE WORLD

This is a book about the end of the world. Or the end of the world as we know it, at least. I can't imagine any more important a subject about which to write a book.

The world will end one day, probably when something dramatic happens in the natural development of the star we call the Sun. It happens to other stars, so I guess it will happen to ours. At some point it will cease functioning as an ordinary, successful star, its supply of hydrogen will run low, and as the inner core contracts and heats up, the outside will cool. This is called the Red Giant stage of a star's life cycle, and as part of the cooling process a large part of the Sun's matter will spin off into space, doing surrounding planets no good at all. However, as the core heats up, the Sun's energy output will have increased a hundredfold. By the time the Sun reaches the next stage in its life, becoming a White Dwarf, any sentient being in the solar system is likely to be well past caring.

The usual scientific estimate of when these events will occur is maybe four thousand million years' time, and while I feel some sympathy for any living creature still around on our planet then, I have no personal worries about that event. The next five years are quite enough for me to deal with.

So, it isn't that end of the world that this book is about. Instead, it's an end of the world that may come as a result of an intervention in the natural course of events, so that the planet does not survive to be ruined by an over-energetic Sun. Or if it does reach that time, the people on it – and little is ever said about the rest of the Earth's living creatures – have long since left, or changed, or are part of a new kind of creation that has taken our place, a creation not victim to the vagaries of the Sun.

I've used the word "intervention", and that is going to be one of our recurring themes. More traditional concepts like "salvation", "punishment", "judgment" and "resurrection" will be there, too, but the idea of an intervention in the normal, natural course of events is probably the key to understanding what this book is about.

A Time of Visions

And not just of visions, but of messages, visitations, discoveries and of inexplicable journeys away from the world. We are looking forward to a day that may come soon, when everything will change, and will change us. The world has never seen so many claims of extraordinary experience as have been made known in the past 20 years, so many reports of information and warnings about our immediate future. All the evidence I've seen recently suggests that the pace of these experiences is still increasing, that more people than ever believe that they know what the future holds for some or all of the human race. The sources of that knowledge are so varied that the consensus between the prophets, channellers, interpreters and scholars of ancient texts can seem quite remarkable. It's natural to ask why there is such agreement that massive change is about to take place, or may even have started.

We have here more and varied prophecies around and about the Millennium than have, to my knowledge, been collected anywhere else. Some are about a final, physical end of this world. Some welcome the prospect of dramatic and disastrous physical changes in the Earth, because there has to be a new beginning for us. Others foresee a wonderful, spiritual change in our consciousness and our attitudes to each other and the world we live in. Yet others think that the future of our race lies in being forced to interbreed with short, grey alien beings from barely visible UFOs. Some prophecies and predictions combine two or three of these elements.

We are, of course, looking for dates. They aren't that common, but we have a fair number. In the historical resources of prophecy we find Nostradamus with July or August 1999, and a Great King of Terror coming from skies. We're told that the architecture of the Great Pyramid reveals that on February 21, 1999 the long-lost, legendary Great Hall of Records will be rediscovered under the Pyramid and Sphinx, changing mankind for ever. The Mayan prophecies suggest cataclysm in 2012, Hopi prophecies even earlier. St Malachy, or somebody using his name, saying there will only be two more Popes, the last of all seeing his flock through a great tribulation, and into the Second Coming of Christ.

From the New Age believers comes Ashtar, assuring us of the landing of 15 million flying saucers, starting in September 1996. Pleiadeans, Arcturans and Sirians promise us Ascension in the next decade, travelling across the universe to link with other space beings in leading humanity to a breakthrough into a higher state of awareness and existence, liaising with the starseed and star children living among us.

The more traditional Christian prophets lead us to believe that the End Times sequence set out in the Book of Revelation is about to begin, or already has. The Rapture of believers may be next year, the Antichrist is already climbing to his position of world domination, the Mark of the Beast will be a computer code or chip under our skin, based round the dreaded numbers 666, and controlling our financial and personal affairs till the end of seven years of misery before the Second Coming. Evangelist David Hathaway believes that Vladimir Zhirinovsky, the Russian politician, is the Antichrist. Michael Callagher thinks the Great Beast may be a giant computer that's controlled by US Vice-President Al Gore, and that the rapture is set for Christmas Day, 1999. Like many others, famous evangelist Hal Lindsey is waiting for the Battle of Armageddon, when the Europeans nuke the Americans, and 200 million Chinese invade Israel across the dried-up bed of the River Euphrates.

The modern prophets look to pole shifts, comets and earthquakes as the route to a better world. Stan Deyo dreams that Australia will soon be where Antarctica is now, covered with ice, and prepares to warn his followers when to take to the mountains. Gordon Michael-Scallion knows how and when California will fracture and become known as the Isles of California, that the post-disaster USA will be organised into 13 colonies, that there will be a nuclear war between 1995 and 1998.

Religious visions appear all over the world, mostly in the form of the Virgin Mary, who warns of the terrible and inevitable results of mankind's behaviour if we do not change our ways, and Russia is not consecrated to Her Immaculate Heart. We still wait to know the truth of the Third Secret of Fatima. Cults risk the lives of themselves and others in the belief that the end times have arrived, and tragedies like the massacre at Waco, the self-immolation of the members of the Order of the Solar Temple, and the mass sarin poisonings by the Aum cult in Japan seem set to repeat themselves.

All this takes place against a background of increasingly strange beliefs and experiences. In the established Christian churches the Toronto Blessing takes a firmer hold, as believers possessed by the spirit they call holy roll around on church floors, laughing and barking. Thousands of reasonable people report that they have been forced to interbreed with aliens, to create a new intergalactic bloodline, and maybe become citizens of a new and different creation, leaving ours behind. There appear to be no limits on the future that may face us.

My intention is to explore all of these wonders, and more, because this is an exciting time, and it demands to be properly reported. If it all seems a little confusing, if there seem to be impossible contradictions between the different prophecies and predictions being made, just remember that nations have fought holy wars over less, and will probably continue to do so. This is a book about what will, if it happens, most probably be the outstanding event of your life. And everybody else's. What more could you ask from a book?

"Millennium" and "Millennial"

At this point, let's clarify a couple of points that seem to confuse most of the media, and many of the rest of us. There's a difference between "millennium" and "millennial" which isn't at all well understood.

A "millennium" is a period of one thousand years, and when we describe the year 2000 as "the millennium" we are really referring to the start of a new millennium, or the end of an old one. When the year 1000 AD arrived, people were in a similar situation, except that our old millennium was their new one. And so on.

The word "millennial", on the other hand, is used to refer to the religions, sects and cults which expect Christ to return to earth, and then to reign here for a period of one thousand years – also a millennium. The belief that Christ will return and reign for a thousand years is often called "millenarianism". Because it is based on the particular expectation of Christ's return, such belief doesn't have to be tied to any particular starting date, and there have been "millenarian" movements throughout the past 1,900 years. There will be further millennial movements in the future. To misquote Charles Fort, you can measure a millennium beginning anywhere.

So, why write this book now? And why read it now? The title gives a partial answer: because there's a Millennium coming up. Humanity becomes excited by numbers of years ending in just one '"nought". We review a past decade, look forward to the next one. We define by decades: the 60s, the 70s, the 80s, using the terms to summarise fashion, attitudes, music, wealth. The organisers of pub theme nights and manufacturers of compilation albums have a lot to answer for. But sometimes these terms describe quite fairly. My influences are definitely 60s ones, my attitudes bear the mark of the ageing urban hippy. You'll spot some of them in my writing.

Being born in 1950, I recall that when I was six or seven years old I actively anticipated how grand it would be to be 50 – a special age – in 2000 – a clearly special year. It's disappointing to see my special year somewhat hijacked by the Government and its Millennium Commission, but I have no doubt that ringing in the New Year of 2000 AD will be an exciting moment.

If, that is, we last even that long. Or if we have long left after that date. Bear in mind, if you would, a warning like the ones given at the end of television programmes showing or re-enacting vicious crimes, usually along the lines of: "Don't lose any sleep, it almost certainly won't happen to you." But there really is a lot of prophecy, prediction and premonition around at present, pointing to, and around the year 2000. Some of that prophecy may date from before the birth of Jesus Christ. Some of it arrives through my front door, day after day. Prophets tend not to be shrinking violets, although it often takes money to encourage them to share their wisdom with people like me.

A Millennium Consensus

The tradition of crossing the palm of the soothsayer with silver dies hard, but by whatever route the wisdom reaches us, much of it persuades me of the reality of what I've started calling the 'Millennium Consensus', which is a handy way of describing the wide range of faiths, cults, belief groups and individuals who foresee some momentous events and astonishing changes in the next three to five years.

As to why you should read this book, aside from the obvious advantage of being prepared for any eventuality, I hope that partly, anyway, it's because you share my fascination with remarkable beliefs and events. No doubt many of you read *Fortean Times* every month, delighting in the worldwide variety of human knowledge, and experience, and inspiration that it reports. The Millennium Consensus offers all that, at its very best.

I hope that you're also trying to understand how and why those reports and experiences come about. While *FT*'s approach may be to find fun in the accounts it publishes, it isn't usually to make fun of the people in those accounts. Not unless they're particularly arrogant, unpleasant, or disagreeable, anyway. But that doesn't mean that we can't try to get under the surface of the messages that the cults and prophets, channellers and interpreters of prophecy are giving to us. You can find quite a selection of books – and we'll assess the value of some of them – which just scratch that surface. The message may be important, or it may be nonsense. Judging by the past performances of prophets, chances are it will probably be wrong. But what is always interesting is the question of where the message has come from, and the authority that the messenger claims to relay that message. What right do individuals think they have to set theselves up to tell us our future? And in most cases, how to conduct ourselves as and till that future unfolds.

There will always be exceptions, but the authority claimed by prophets usually takes one of three forms. First, there is the straightforward interpretation of existing information or data. This is generally a book or text of some kind, but is sometimes a building, like the Great Pyramid, a Mayan stone carving, a painting, even a crop circle, or the layout of a landscape like that round the mysterious Rennes-le-Chateau.

Second, there is what might be called 'guided interpretation', where an individual uses similar information or data to the above, but credits another – usually non-human – intelligence with guiding, inspiring, or simply providing their understanding. This may be directly, by a visit from an angel or other heavenly or mystical being, or simply by a method like automatic writing.

Third, and increasingly common, there is the type of information and data said to come directly from non-human intelligences, regardless of existing texts or other clues. In these cases, the messenger often takes on the role of medium or, more recently, channeller. It may be claimed that the information has been received during some altered state of consciousness, during an out-of-body or near-death experience, for instance, or a visit to heaven or another planet. Yes, it's an old role, but with a new twist. And it's one which has produced a vast amount of prophecy for the coming Millennium.

Non-Human Intelligences

This is a good point at which to talk about what I mean by "non-human intelligences". I've found that this is a useful tag to describe a vast range of supposed beings who aren't human and aren't, in terms of breathing, eating, going to the toilet and so on, alive. They are, however, capable of independent, intelligent thought and often display a fair degree of self-determination, although frequently they appear to be the minions and messengers of others. Because I use the expression to include every sort of non-human being from the Jehovah of the Old Testament, to the humblest demon, from the Archangel Michael and Ashtar and all his Command, to somebody's great uncle who died last Friday and has apparently returned with a message through a Spiritualist medium, I've found that I can succeed in offending more or less anybody. But if it thinks, and interacts, and it isn't a live human being, then so far as I'm concerned it's an non-human intelligence. If it isn't love that makes the world go round, it's probably something to do with the NHIs.

So, this isn't another pot-boiler, throwing together a few spooky prophecies and premonitions to give you something to glance through on the bus. My plan here is to go a lot further than that. Not only to tell you about the messenger and the message, but also the source of the information, the way it's received, and what the messenger does to make it known. If there are prophecies which are more likely to tell us more about our future than we can work out from the interpretation of straightforward scientific information, these are key factors to consider.

Chapter 2

APOCALYPSE, PLAGUE AND JUDGMENT

Christianity isn't the only religion that has clear ideas about the end of the world, and about God's role in it. But the Christian idea of how that end will come about is the foundation of many of the prophecies in this book. Early Christians set out the different stages and elements that are expected to take place on the way to the second coming and the other Millennium – the thousand years of Christ's reign on Earth with his chosen people. Although far away in time, it's vital to know how these expectations came about, and what they are. And as we consider more modern, unfulfilled prophecies – prophecies for our own time – we may ask why these same expectations keep repeating themselves so regularly, only changing and adapting to fit in with life at the time that each of them is made?

The events the Bible predicts will take place at the end of the world are meant to seem horrifyingly real. They've stoked the imaginations of believers for 2,000 years, and when you hear talk of 'fire and brimstone' preachers, this is the material. Should they happen as promised – or threatened – the suffering caused will make the World Wars pale into insignificance. The divinely-inflicted sickness will randomly kill more individuals than all the plagues in history. AIDS will be overshadowed. The terror promised in the Bible, and particularly in its last book, Revelation, leaves me wondering how any thinking person can believe that a loving God would treat His creation in that way. But the prophecies, and the promises, have been made. The Biblical 'End Times' scenario underlies much of the later prophecy and prediction for the Millennium. Many of the prophecies for the Millennium throw around expressions like the Rapture, the Antichrist, Great Beast, Mark of the Beast, the Second Coming, and the Last Judgment. All these have their roots in the Bible, and to understand millennial prophecy, we need to know what was promised in the Bible, and how the words and expressions used there have been interpreted since those promises were made.

The prophecies that concern us are made in two of the most difficult, important and influential books of the Bible. The Book of Daniel, from the Old Testament, and the Revelation of St John the Divine, the final book in the Bible, have set the pattern for many of the messages given by other, later prophets and interpreters. These two books present us not only with remarkable prophecies, and accounts of extraordinary visions. They also explain what may be the most profound interventions in the world's affairs.

Now, some people have always seen visions, and dreamed dreams, and made contact with a wide range of Non-Human Intelligences. That isn't a fact that most believers like to come to terms with because one of the attractions of being a visionary, of receiving a message that you feel responsible for passing on, is that it makes you special, and important.

But I'm confident that this kind of experience is currently reaching a surprising new peak, and that this involves an unprecedented degree of expectation about dramatic changes coming in the next few years. This is a remarkable time for extraordinary experiences. Still, acknowledging that other people are having equally exciting and dramatic experiences, when their messages are different to yours, isn't easy. It just isn't how most human beings respond.

I've met and talked at length with people who've experienced visions and visitations of all kinds, and researched hundreds more incidents that are said to have taken place over more than one thousand years of human history. I've learned that the trick is to look at similar experiences whenever, and wherever they occur. Looking at one type of vision, or one or two individuals in isolation, tells you very little indeed.

So, when I come to assess the significance of Daniel, and of Revelation, I do it bearing all those other experiences in mind. I don't start with the belief that what is included in any one version of the Bible is the Word of God. Quite apart from the number of gods whose words are currently in circulation, there are so many different versions of the Bible, including and excluding various books and documents according to taste, that the Word of God would have to vary accordingly. And more than that, Revelation in particular had a pretty difficult ride on the way to being included in the New Testament. It could have been left out entirely, and only by the choice of certain influential individuals and groups did it achieve its current position. It is, still, substantially ignored by most mainstream church people. In all the years that I was an active member of the Church of England, I can't recall a single reading in church of any part of Revelation other than the messages to local churches that start the book off. When I came to read theology at university, it was still a mystery to me, and I think I was typical of most Christians.

For me, there's only two ways to look at the authors of Daniel, and of Revelation. We don't really know who, individually, wrote either, so I won't be specific. One is to treat them as writers assuming the cloak of visionary experience as a sort of fictional style for conveying complicated ideas and beliefs about the nature of reality and the future. The other is to treat them as visionaries and prophets, who wrote down the detail of experiences they genuinely felt they had been through, during which they received information from God – and various other intelligences of a religious persuasion – about, well, the nature of reality and the future.

The first of these options has a lot of support. There has long been a literary form known as 'apocalyptic' in which a legendary or famous person of the past is reported as having had strange experiences in which they received information about the future by non-conventional means. Confusingly, this meant that it was quite acceptable for apocalyptic to be written after some or all of the events it appeared to predict had occurred. Less confusingly, the reason for this was usually that it was designed to encourage and support the Jewish nation when it was oppressed and disheartened, which was often the case. If God could be shown to care about His people to the extent that He had appeared to the 'legendary or famous person' to predict the future, and that prediction related to changes favourable to the Jews, that had to be a good sign. I can see why apocalyptic works are written that way; propaganda and public relations are nothing new. Giving comfort to those who need it is nothing new. Telling little, or even fairly big, white lies has a tremendous historical pedigree.

The Book of Daniel

The Book of Daniel was probably written between 100 and 200 BC, when Judaism was under attack by Antiochus IV of Syria. He plundered the treasure of the temple in Jerusalem, prevented the Jews from observing the Sabbath and performing other requirements of their religion, and set up a statue of Zeus in the Temple, enforcing pagan patterns of worship. It was a time of severe oppression. The author of Daniel – the name may come from earlier mythology, and nobody would actually have expected it to be the author's real name – set his story some 400 years in the past, although some fundamentalists, such as Hal Lindsey insist that it was written exactly when the word of the Bible says it was.

The book's content centres round a prophecy of Judaism being oppressed, but achieving better times just as that prophecy had suggested, with the fall of the Babylonian empire of King Nebuchadnezzar. On this occasion, the prophecies emerge from 'Daniel' interpreting a dream experienced by Nebuchadnezzar, and then of explaining the meaning of complex dreams or visions he had experienced himself.

The popular stories in Daniel, the ones that most people remember, are of Shadrach, Meshach and Abednego in the burning, fiery furnace, of the events at King Belshazzar's feast, and of Daniel in the lion's den. All good supernatural stuff. But the Bible itself appears to make no pretence that these were historical events. There is no evidence of any recollection of these events being passed down for 400 years before they were first recorded in writing. The 'date verses' in Daniel, which specify various calculations of days and years for the fulfilment of various prophecies have kept interpreters, and more modern prophets, busy for more than 2,000 years. As we'll come to expect, the days aren't real days, or the years real years, except where they are, but it is on these verses most of the specific predictions of a Christian end of the world have been based. Daniel looks unmistakably 'apocalyptic', probably put together for entirely proper motives, but not intended to be accepted as objective truth even when written, let alone more than 2,000 years later. Our ancestors seem to have grasped the idea of parables and symbolic stories much better than many modern Christians.

Revelation

At the time Daniel was written, the apocalyptic form was relatively new, and the Book of Daniel was the most recognisable form of the style to date. The Book of Revelation was written more than 200 years later and by then the style was well established. A more dramatic and complicated work, it presents a very gory, definitively Christian 'End Times Scenario', and predicts specific events leading up to the Last Judgment. It contains material that clearly fits the description 'apocalyptic', and has been described as being unfortunately disjointed because it contains undiluted chunks of traditional forms of apocalyptic writings borrowed from elsewhere. But is it all just that, or is there a real vision, a real experience, hidden away in this extraordinary book? And if there is, what significance did it have? And what significance does it have for the future?

The Revelation of St John is the last book of the standard Christian Bible. The Bible is the most published book in the history of western civilisation, and probably the most influential. I could make an argument for Revelation being the most influential book in the Bible, and as the year 2000 approaches my case would grow stronger. Revelation has introduced concepts about the nature and prevalence and intrusion of evil into the world and its human occupants that have no parallel in any other literature. It has defined a pattern for the events that will lead up to the Second Coming of Christ, and the Last Judgment. It makes promises that are nowhere else made with such force, and are often made nowhere else at all. It has had, and still has, a greater effect on human behaviour in the western world than any other single piece of writing. Concepts, words, names and events that originated with the author of Revelation appear in a remarkably high proportion of the prophecies and predictions gathered together in this book.

Revelation recounts a vision of the end of life on earth as we know it, and the horrors that sections of mankind will have to suffer, first one section for being loyal to Jesus Christ, then another for being disloyal to Him. It was undoubtedly written in the belief that the end of the world events it described were not the best part of 2,000 years away. The date it was written is uncertain, but probably lies somewhere between 65AD and 100AD when the events described were of personal importance to the writer and his readers. They expected that at least some of their number would be alive when the events took place.

The debate about the identity of the man who wrote Revelation is much too lengthy to go into here. There's a possibility it was the same John that wrote the Gospel, but a probability it wasn't. It may have been someone else called John or, as we know happened with other apocalyptic writings, it may not. The events it refers to appear to have occured on the Aegean island of Patmos, but the early history of the book itself is very vague indeed, and the first clear reference to the identity of the author doesn't come till around 135 AD. The disagreements have hardly stopped from that time on.

Yet we don't need to know who the author was to assess the value of the book. Taken at face value, the vision it reports must have been a terrifying one. It has formed a pattern for the content of many later visions, but it does have a grandeur all of its own. I know a smidgeon of New Testament Greek, but I'm completely dependent on scholars and linguists, not only for their ability to translate accurately the complex images and descriptions of Revelation, but also to tell me what the images and symbols mean. This in itself leads to confusion at times, like where some lampstands represent churches, and in the extraordinary array of beasts with physical attributes borrowed from all over the natural world, that do things that no ordinary beast would ever be expected to, because they are designed to represent people, places and civilisations known well to the author of Revelation, but an absolute mystery to us. The content of Revelation has much in common with the prophecies of Nostradamus – a determined interpreter can find pretty much what he or she wants somewhere in the words and symbols, because they are so exotic, and so unrelated to events that occur in the real world.

A few brief passages illustrate the point, taken from throughout the vision and prophecy sections of Revelation:

"I looked, and behold a door was opened in heaven... and immediately I was in the spirit, and behold a throne was set in heaven, and one sat on the throne... and there was a rainbow round about the throne in sight like unto an emerald... and in the midst of the throne and round about the throne were four beasts full of eyes before and behind... and I heard the voice of many angels about the throne and the beasts and the elders, and the number of them was ten thousand times ten thousand, and thousands of thousands."

"And I looked and behold a pale horse, and his name that on him was death, and Hell followed with him. And power was given to them over the fourth part of the earth, to kill with sword, and with hunger, and with death, and with the beasts of the earth... and the heaven departed as a scroll when it is rolled together: and every mountain and island were moved out of their places."

"And the third angel sounded, and there fell a great star from heaven... and the name of the star is called Wormwood: and the third part of the waters became wormwood: and many men died because they were made bitter... and to them (the locusts) it was given that they should not kill them, but that they should be tormented five months. and the shapes of the locusts were like unto horses prepared into battle."

"Here is wisdom. Let him that hath understanding count the number of the beast: for it is the number of a man; and his number is six hundred three-score and six."

On that last point – the Number of the Beast – all the serious, scholarly, religious books I have read have no doubt that this referred to the particular "number", calculated by the system of gematria – giving a numerical value to letters, and adding those numbers in a particular way – of a contemporary oppressor of the early Christians. 666 was a standard calculation of the "number" of the Emperor Nero, and the likelihood is that it was Nero to which this reference applied. Of course, the contemporary readers of Revelation would have known this, and would have agreed with the identification made by "John". They would, I think, have been astonished to find the same calculation applied, well over one thousand years later, to Napoleon, Hitler, Mikhail Gorbachev, Al Gore and a variety of computers. Actually, I suspect they'd have been seriously disappointed to have known that the Second Coming hadn't taken place long before now.

The mention of the Great Beast brings me to the real strength of Revelation, and to acknowledging that whoever wrote it really knew his stuff with regard to creating images and scenarios that would take their place in popular culture, and probably remain there forever. The terms the Great Beast, the Four Horsemen of the Apocalypse, and the Battle of Armageddon – from the reference to events on the Plain of Megiddo – all make their first appearance in Revelation. And just think what we would have missed without them. Who would remember an unsuccessful magician and channeller called Aleister Crowley if he hadn't contrived to make himself known as the Great Beast? What would Albrecht Durer have done for subjects for his woodcuts without those wonderful Horsemen? What might the history of cinema have lost had the scintillating series of *Omen* films not been made?

Other more subtle images and visionary conventions also have their first airing in Revelation. Or maybe not their first airing, but the first that has survived through ages when so little was recorded in writing, and so much that has met destruction at the hands of religious authorities and other censors who found that the easiest way to ensure that their version of true belief survived was to destroy the records of all the others. As I've mentioned, Revelation had something of a charmed life in securing a place not only in the Bible, but as its last book, pointing the way to the future.

Had I been an investigator into extraordinary events on the Isle of Patmos in around 90 AD, and been called in by the local paper to give my opinion on the origin and importance of the document that would later become the Book of Revelation, what would I have made of it? What would you have thought, had you been in that position? I know that I would have considered why it might have been written. Was it, perhaps, simply because eager and respected early Christians wanted to encourage the early churches, to whom Revelation is initially addressed, to maintain their efforts, to conduct themselves well, to keep on believing and sharing their beliefs. That could have been done as well by making the visions up as by them really happening, and the apocalyptic tradition was, after all, one of making things up.

I'd have been concerned about the amount of old material included in Revelation, and wondered why, if God had really made many things known to "John", there had to be so much padding. I'd have been concerned about the predictions of suffering and gloom and mass destruction, promised through all kinds of cruel means by a God that I'd so far understood was meant to be a God of love. Above all, I'd have looked for some evidence that any of the events had the slightest reality or visibility outside the mind of the man who'd written them down. Which is exactly the kind of evidence I'd look for now, in that situation. I think it's reasonable to set aside preconceptions about the importance of the message, and to consider the author of Revelation on a similar basis to those who claim to have been abducted and interfered with by alien beings, or report lengthy conversations with a Virgin Mary who turns up, like clockwork, on a daily or weekly basis, to share the secrets of the universe with somebody who is least well equipped to pass them on.

I can't be sure, but I do suspect that I'd have had some admiration for "John". He was probably trying to do what he believed to be best for a faith and a people to which he was so committed that he had ended up on this island in exile, cut off from the real business of spreading the word. But I don't think I'd have been convinced by his vision, any more than by a hundred others I might have investigated in preceding years. And I'm no more convinced, and no less respectful now, close on 2,000 years later.

Supernatural events are hard to imagine. Most of us who belong to one faith or another accept the accounts of past wonders and miracles without too much bother. They are history, probably part truth, part legend, part symbol and metaphor, and they present no challenge to our belief or disbelief. This is particularly true of a faith based almost entirely in historical events and writings, as is Christianity.

Chapter 3

THE CHRISTIAN END TIMES

Eschatologists – those who deal in the matter of the End Times – are notorious for disagreeing with each other, so the first event in the Bible scenario is not always understood to be the first event that will actually occur: it rather depends on just how much suffering a particular eschatologist considers that faithful Christians should face. However, the End Times are usually expected to begin with the Rapture, which comes before the beginning of the seven years period of Tribulation – though some do place the Rapture halfway through the Tribulation, or even after it finishes. Wherever it is placed, the prospect of this extraordinary event presents a real challenge to the belief or disbelief of almost anyone. It may also provide a truly ancient origin for much more modern beliefs involving rescue, salvation and abduction by airborne entities. Bear that thought in mind as we consider The Rapture.

Getting carried away – the Rapture

The chronology problems over the place of the Rapture in the order of events arise from the "dates verses" in the book of Daniel, but the references to the nature of the Rapture itself are comparatively clear. The key passage is verses 13-18 of Chapter 4 of the First Letter of Paul to the Thessalonians. Concerned that, when Christ returns, the Christians who have already died will be treated differently to those who are currently alive, the writer explains,

"For this we tell you on the Lord's word: we who are left alive until the Lord comes shall not forestall those who have died; because at the word of command, at the sound of the Archangel's voice and God's trumpet call, the Lord himself will descend from Heaven; first the Christian dead will rise, then we who are left alive shall join them, caught up in clouds to meet the Lord in the air. Thus shall we always be with the Lord."

The same writer makes similar points in his Letters to the Corinthians and Hebrews. Indeed, it could be said that popular belief that the Rapture will occur depends substantially on this one individual, and his concept of the future, much as the author of Revelation had his particular ideas about the Great Beast, the Four Horsemen, and the Battle of Armageddon. One individual can make a vast difference to what those who follow him believe to be true. From these origins, various Christian books and pamphlets comment on how the Rapture will actually happen:

"Not one unconverted person will be amongst these greatly privileged people… this coming of our Lord is in the air, and not a coming to the earth, which the writer believes takes place some time later"

"The removal of the Church from the world will doubtless be little more than a 'nine days wonder', but it will mark the withdrawal also of the present restraint upon sin provided by the presence of the Christian."

"He is coming to meet all true believers in the air. Without benefit of science, space suits, or interplanetary rockets, there will be those who will be transported into a glorious place more beautiful, more awesome, than we can possibly comprehend… It will be the living end, the ultimate trip…"

The idea of the Rapture comes over well in fictionalised form. Here are quotes from three intriguing novels dealing with the End Times, the first coming from Sydney Watson's *The Mark of the Beast*, published in 1918:

"Where?" smiled Bastin.

"I don't think anybody knows where, sir!"

"I do, Charley, and many others today who have been left behind from that great Translation know – they have been 'caught up' into the air where Jesus Christ had come from Heaven to summon them to himself. Mr Hammond's there, Charley, and that sweet little adopted daughter of mine, whom you once asked me whether angels could be more beautiful than she was!"

Secondly, from the best-selling *666* by Salem Kirban, published in 1970.

"Just then, Bill shouted excitedly, "George, look out that window. I tell you that's not just a cloud. I've never seen the sky so funny looking. It's as though it was opening up… George IT IS OPENING UP… PEELING BACK LIKE A SCROLL. George, what's happening?"

And then it happened… It seemed like the plane got much lighter, turned abruptly and went into a dive from 80,000 feet high… There had been two stewardesses standing next to me, but when I awoke only one was there!… Just then, the intercom came on and we heard a voice. "Ladies and gentlemen, something rather unusual has happened... our pilot has vanished."

(The stewardess) pointed with trembling hands. 'LOOK", she screamed, 'HALF OF THE PASSENGERS ARE MISSING!' I'll never forget the chills that ran up and down my spine. It wasn't half, but it looked as though 100 or so just disappeared. And I turned to tell Bill. BUT BILL WASN'T THERE!

And suddenly it came to me... I WAS HERE."

You can read some rather sordid discussion about the fate of babies and young children when the Rapture takes place. If they are not Christians, will they be left to suffer the horrors of the Tribulation, quite possibly without their parents. The majority opinion appears to be that "unsaved children" or "unconverted children" will be taken, but the Bible doesn't make that clear, and there are certainly eschatologists who think otherwise. It's an issue that can bring home the full horror of prophesied events becoming real events, real events such as the Great Tribulation.

Seven years of Hell on Earth

Human beings are very good at writing about hell, and hopelessly bad at writing about heaven. They make a horribly thorough job of speculating about the Tribulation, too. This rather sad situation has, I suspect, come about because we know of bad things that have happened to us and to other people, and we only need to exaggerate them to present a viable picture of hell. Heaven often seems like a very dull prospect indeed. Harps, clouds, hymns, and interminable cries of "Holy, Holy, Holy". That sort of thing. While the promise of peace may be a wonderful prospect for individuals or peoples who have none – and that's behind a lot of millennial hope and expectation, after all – I'm sure I'm not alone in being unexcited by the prospect. It's hard to imagine anything endlessly pure and holy being any fun. If someone told me that heaven would offer me a chance to carry on the best relationships I have here on earth I'd be a lot more impressed, but important issues like that never seem to get a mention.

Anyway, the Tribulation is really nasty. Unless you happen to have been raptured beforehand – and remember, some of the authorities predict that the Rapture won't happen till during or after the Tribulation – there's suffering for everybody over a seven-year spread. This is, as you can imagine, drawn mainly from Daniel and Revelation, and it has become the centre of some of the most unpleasant and divisive speculation you can imagine.

The Tribulation period includes the "Seven Trumpets" from Revelation 8, and the "Seven Vials" from Revelation 16. Read the originals to see what a bleak and heartless vision this really was. The trumpets bring hail, fire and blood falling down on the earth. One-third of the world's trees and grass disappear. One-third of the sea turns to blood. The mysterious falling star Wormwood – which probably isn't really linked with the original meaning of the name Chernobyl, in spite of recent speculation – poisons the seas and rivers. Sun, moon and stars go dark. Something like 200 million soldiers on horseback breathing fire and brimstone slaughter one-third of mankind, while huge locust-cum-horse-cum-scorpion beings torment those who have not been "sealed" by God.

The political events of the world are dominated by mythical creatures and entities. I guess it's possible that may be an improvement, but during the first half of the seven years, two "witnesses" turn water into blood, devastate the world with plague, and cause massive drought, till a beast – not the "Great Beast" but a somewhat lesser one – comes out of a bottomless pit and kills them, leading to their resurrection three-and-a-half days later. A battle in heaven involving a mysterious woman "clothed with the sun" (and often identified with the Virgin Mary), her male child, a seven-headed, ten-horned red dragon, and Michael and the angels, results in the dragon (Satan) and his angels (angels aren't necessarily good) ending up on earth.

The Mark of the Beast

A beast of similar description, but with elements of leopard, lion and bear, comes out of the sea to become the Great Beast who we've mentioned before, although he seems to have little in common with either Aleister Crowley or, indeed, the British UFO contactee who told me he was the Great Beast when I first met him 15 or more years ago. Anyway, this beast has another beast to help him (I hope you're following this), who is traditionally referred to as the False Prophet, and between the two of them they undertake the whole "Mark of the Beast" scenario. Basically, everyone who wants to buy or sell goods – particularly food – is expected to have a mark on their right hand or forehead in order to do so. This leads to those faithful Christians who weren't good enough to be raptured having a miserable time because they refuse to bear the Mark.

The Mark is usually associated with 666, the "number of the Beast", and not surprisingly, as computers have become more accessible, and barcodes on goods commonplace in much of the world, speculation about the Mark centres round computers. Old illustrations of the Mark show frightened people with the figures "666" stamped on their foreheads or hands, but that never seemed to make any sense. The concept of a minute barcode, or even more likely an implanted computer chip, does make the Mark a more practical possibility. A brilliant account of this period of the Tribulation is given in the Christian novel, The Seven Last Years, by Carol Balizet, which seems to have been distributed by a number of different publishers.

Matters become very complicated now, with the Lamb of God, elders, beasts, harpists, singers and 144,000 redeemed saints appearing on (a presumably very crowded) Mount Zion. There are descriptions of the punishments for those who gave in and took the Mark of the Beast, and some unpleasant assertions of blood coming out of a sort of "human winepress", covering an area of 1600 furlongs. If you wanted to frighten people into behaving themselves, you could hardly do it better. Then it's time for the Seven Vials.

If you were involved in the sort of planning for natural disasters undertaken by governments and local authorities here and in most of the developed world, you'd probably have given up and gone home long ago. If you hadn't, the Seven Vials would be the last straw. More hailstones, earthquakes, noisome and grievous sores, vanishing mountains and islands, a scorching sun, the sea like a dead man's blood, unclean spirits like frogs, the drying-up of the River Euphrates. And, of course, the beginning of revenge on those who had been so unwise as to accept the Mark.

Second Coming, Armageddon and Judgment

By the end of this sequence, everything is set up for the Battle at Armageddon, with the Kings of the Earth gathered on the Plain of Megiddo. The Whore of Babylon appears, and ten kings make war with the Lamb who appeared on Zion. They are defeated, Babylon falls, and eventually Jesus Christ, soldier and political leader for this, his Second Coming, comes to earth on a white horse, and the massive last battle takes place. Beast and False Prophet end up in that well-publicised version of hell, being "cast alive into a lake of fire burning with brimstone", and the followers of the Beast – those who took the Mark and didn't repent in time – are murdered with swords and their bodies and bones picked over by birds. Satan is sealed in the bottomless pit for the 1,000 years that form the Christian version of the Millennium, while back on earth Christ reigns over a world populated by those who resisted the Beast and suffered for their faith during the Tribulation.

The end of the sequence is covered very briefly – it's that problem about describing heaven again, no easier when trying to describe heaven on earth – but it looks as though Satan is let out of the bottomless pit, only to be thoroughly thrashed again. Then it is time for the last judgment, the dead leave their graves, and everyone who has ever lived on the planet finds themselves either in the joy of an eternal "new heaven and a new earth", or consigned to some hell. No way out, no second chances.

A HISTORY OF FAILURE?

I don't find it easy to imagine myself into the minds of people in history. Over the years, I've investigated events that happened before Egyptian times, but once I've reached back more than 150 years or so the people I write about seem not only like strangers, but like complete aliens. More than that, having led a generally stable, middle-class life here in the safety of England, it's not easy to identify with people who have suffered extreme poverty, slavery, oppression or worse.

Which makes it difficult for me to understand what has driven most of the leaders and followers of end times movements over the past couple of thousand years. What do I know of how it felt to be a Christian when the Book of Revelation was written, a member of one of a few scattered groups, living in a desperate confusion of hope and fear? Hoping for the imminent return of Jesus Christ, fulfilling all the promises to those who believe in him, but fearing what the civil authorities might do to me, facing exile, prison, even death. What do I know about being so poor that I can see no prospect of anything other than misery for me or my family unless some higher power intervenes, either changing the circumstances of my life here, or taking me off to another place to be happy and safe forever? How can I identify with somebody whose desperation leads him or her to put their faith and their future in the hands of somebody who, to anyone able to look calmly and objectively at the situation, is plainly an exploiter, a user, a thief, and quite possibly a murderer, too?

Which isn't to say that I haven't tried. Trying to understand all these circumstances is important. It's easy enough to mock cults and those who believe in them. Look at current attitudes to the Moonies, the Children of God, the Jesus Army, the Hare Krishna movement. How many of you were once devotees of Transcendental Meditation, or the Divine Light Mission and Guru Maharaj Ji? What made you think that you were in touch with something special? Did you really believe that rubbing your eyes very hard had anything to do with God, or linked you with some remarkable, mystical reality? How did others regard your beliefs then? And how do you look back on those times now that you're older and possibly wiser?

Now, in the Western world, relatively few people join cults and belief groups because of their grinding, physical poverty. Few face systematic, state-driven political oppression. Few people in Europe, North America or Australia have to fear for their lives or their freedom because of their religious beliefs, although sadly there are far too many other parts of the world where that is exactly the case. Yet we still find end times beliefs of all kinds appearing in countries where those pressures seldom, if ever, arise. I suspect that these modern beliefs are motivated by different feelings and experiences to those that inspired many of the beliefs of the past. Are there real differences between people who are driven into beliefs of dramatic and irrevocable change by the harshness of their lives and the bleakness of their futures, and those who appear to come to hold similar beliefs, who make similar prophecies by choice, without being driven to them by the same old fears? Can we work out what those differences might be?

Sadly, most accounts of those who have predicted the end of the world have long since been packaged by historians into neat little presentations that completely fail to capture the sheer emotional fervour they must really have had. There isn't much I can do about that, without several spare years and an understanding of a range of extinct languages. Even then I'd have that problem of identifying with the people I was writing about. I guess that's one of the reasons why I'm trying to make a decent job of recording what's going on now.

What we have left of most of the past is what looks like a record of almost total failure: a simple sequence of events, repeated over and again. Somebody comes up with a prophecy, people follow him (or occasionally her), the prophecy fails, the people disperse and go off to believe in something else. I could produce a list, a catalogue even, of these failures in specific prophecy, when the great, dramatic, heavenly event doesn't happen as it has been promised. Just the ones that have been written down, and which I've come across in my research run to hundreds in the past 2,000 years. There are probably many others about which we'll never even know. Think of my own personal visionary, and my own, personal Jesus Christ. How many times over do these things happen?

So, let's forget about making a catalogue of failure, and try to look at some of the people of the past, and their prophecies. 1,800 years of promises and disappointments.

To 1000 AD

Social and political situations often set the tone of faith and prophecy, and as early as 45 AD, a man called Theudas led a large group of Jews to follow him to the shores of the River Jordan, telling them it would part to let them cross. They were captured by the Roman authorities, and the prophecy was never tested. Then around 172 AD the prophet Montanus gained a strong following in North Africa, Asia Minor and parts of Europe. He said that he himself was the Holy Spirit, that the Last Judgment was imminent, and that the New Jerusalem would descend, ready built, in Phrygia, where he lived.

As early as 426 AD, St Augustine was trying to persuade other influential churchmen not to give dates for events prophesied as happening in the future, but nothing could stop interpretation, the trick of looking at dramatic current events and concluding that the end was close. The persistence of plagues and famines in France was recognised as a sign of the End Times in 591, when a messiah calling himself Christ, travelling with a woman called Mary, raised what was virtually an army of believers before being defeated by the forces of an opposing bishop. Similar messiahs and end-times prophets grew out of the harshness of peasant life in following years.

In 740, proving that nothing is new in the field of contact with non-human intelligences, a messiah called Aldebert had contacts with various angels, including one who could bring him relics from all over the world with which he could work miracles. He performed healings, claimed he was holy when born, and that he had some of Christ's powers. He at least died a fairly natural death, more than can be said for many of those who went off on the Crusades a few hundred years later, often believing that when they conquered Jerusalem the end times cycle would begin, and they would be particularly blessed for their part in it. The cruelty and bigotry of the Crusades make me wonder whether any one who took an active part in them ever made it up to heaven at all, despite all the promises made to them before they set out.

New Year's Eve, 999

1000 AD ought to have been something very special, and there is a sort of accepted wisdom what about happened on the day before the last millennium ended – New Year's Eve, 999 AD. On the basis that Revelation predicted that Satan would be unleashed 1,000 years on from the birth of Christ, and that the reappearance of Satan would trigger the end of the world, millions of Christians are supposed to have been stricken with anxious expectation, involved in the ultimate countdown to the end of the world.

Pope Sylvester II is credited with hosting a dramatic service in St Peter's in Rome, and the Christians of Europe are supposed to have given away their land, their homes and their possessions. Debts are said to have been cancelled, crimes confessed to, and people to have tried to put their spiritual affairs in order by the old-fashioned techniques of self-mortification – uncomfortable underwear, stones in your shoes, that kind of thing. The social norms had been defied with the liberation of farm animals, the release of prisoners, the feeding of beggars, and shops giving food away for nothing.

In Jerusalem (then a Moslem city), people were supposed to have filled the streets. In a strange anticipation of both religious visionaries and UFO watchers of future years, it is said that they were trying to reach an unspecified spot where they expected the returning Christ to land. In Rome, many of Pope Sylvester's congregation were apparently clad in sackcloth and ashes when, as the legend goes, "the giant clock ticking away the last minutes of the first millennium suddenly stopped. Not a few died from fright, giving up their ghosts then and there. But after an awful moment that seemed like eternity suspended, the clock resumed its countdown. Only the ominous tick – tock and the voice of the Pope broke the deathly silence. Sylvester chanted the sacred Latin phrases, and at precisely midnight the bells atop the great tower began to peal wildly, The Te Deum was sung. And no fire fell from Heaven."

I'm no expert on clocks, but I somehow doubt that in 999 there were many publicly ticking away. That aside, there actually seems to be little evidence to support this version of events. I don't know to what extent people were aware of dates, but I'm sure they had no watches, few clocks, no papers, no radios nor televisions. There were no printed Bibles, nor any other books, and such versions of the Book of Revelation as there were would almost all have been locked away in religious establishments. It's suggested that the cultural output of monasteries and other religious houses – where religious works were painstakingly reproduced by hand – dropped over the last 50 years before the Millennium, perhaps because it really wasn't worth putting in all the painstaking effort of copying out page after page of any book if the world was ending. I do wonder whether the vast majority of people cared about an obscure section of a part of the Bible they neither knew nor understood?

There isn't much of a historical record to suggest that they did. There is no mention of any relevant events in the section on Millenarianism in *The Oxford Dictionary of the Christian Church* or in Kenneth Scott Latourette's *A History of Christianity*. The 16-volume *Encyclopedia of Religion*, edited by Mircea Eliade, has a long section on millennial beliefs, written by Hillel Schwartz. This covers 1000 AD succinctly, saying, "...no millenarian movements and exceedingly few prophecies were geared to the year 1000 (few then used such a calendar)." I suspect that Schwartz may have it about right.

Moving on some years, Joachim of Fiore was among the prophets of the Crusaders. He prophesied to Richard the Lionheart that Saladin was the Antichrist predicted in the Book of Revelation, and that Richard would defeat him. This prophecy was not fulfilled, but Joachim's influence was great, particularly when he linked the Antichrist, and all kinds of anti-Christian activities, to the Jews of Europe. Among those he influenced was Frederick II of Germany, who took Jerusalem and pronounced himself its ruler in 1229. He was sometimes known as the "Emperor of the Last Days", and after he died in 1250 rumours began that he would be resurrected and return to lead his people. These rumours are still current several hundred years later, and are similar to those about King Arthur in Britain.

The apocalyptic of despair

The famine and disease of the Middle Ages, and the persecution of the Jews across Europe led to substantial millennial movements that grew up as much because of poverty and oppression as because of visions and prophecies. Many of these groups formed around leaders whose sanity and motives both seemed to be questionable, and as has happened many times since, those leaders placed little value on the life and death of their followers. These movements often started with a charismatic leader promising a unique salvation and a future social position to his, and occasionally her, followers. But once the group – sometimes thousands strong – had established itself in a town or district, the new social order would just involve new masters for the poor, and self-appointed kingship and wealth for the leader. Movements of this kind still emerge from time to time – some of the richer gurus of the past 20 years come to mind, particularly one associated with the colour orange. But perhaps they weren't really prophetic movements, because they didn't base their activities and hopes round any particular End Times scenario.

Several books have been filled with movements of this kind, and they make fascinating reading. The ability of human beings not only to believe in the most peculiar assertions, but to live them out as well, is shown in action in the unpleasant "self-flagellation" movement that started in European monasteries in the eleventh century, and lasted for hundreds of years. Nor is the use of Christian belief to justify extreme sexual and social behaviour a recent invention. What was known as the heresy of the "Free Spirit", or "Spiritual Liberty", functioned for more than 400 years. It made a virtue of complete immorality, challenging all sexual and social conventions on the basis that the adept had attained total perfection and was incapable of sin. Whatever the act, if an adept performed it, then it couldn't be sinful. Eat your heart out, Aleister Crowley!

There were those who followed Hans Bohm, the Drummer of Niklashausen, in the late 1400s. He had been visited by the Virgin Mary, who gave him a "message of prodigious importance", with the result that his followers found themselves fighting minor wars on behalf of their Messiah. So did the followers of Thomas Muntzer in Bohemia, 40 years later. The many people who put their trust in the Anabaptists under the influential Jan Bockelson in Munster found themselves not in the care of a loving and giving Christ on earth, but with as wicked a tyrant as they could have found anywhere, who used and exploited them ruthlessly.

Intriguing as these groups are, and although all offered one strange end times scenario or another, there are differences between those movements and the kind of future prophecy and worldwide change that this book is about. If you want to read some remarkable accounts of what people choose to believe in, and what they will go through for the promise of even the most outlandish promise of salvation and superiority over others, the material is fascinating. But I suspect that these movements were mostly a result of the times and places where they occurred. Although individuals often claimed to have had visions and visitations from non-human intelligences, many of those claims seemed to be in the tradition of finding a kind of authority for a message a person has decided to give, rather than a genuine personal experience. The leaders would probably have had a lot in common with Charles Manson, Jim Jones, or David Koresh, because if you want to indulge in outlandish or unacceptable behaviour, whether you're robbing your followers or sleeping with their wives, there's no better excuse for doing it than saying that God told you that you could. Unless it's that God told you that you had to: God seems to have done a lot of that sort of thing in the past, and apparently still does sometimes. The Nine O'clock Service in Sheffield could be a very relevant example.

William Miller

Out of all the millennial movements from before the current century, one is particularly prominent, particularly appealing. I guess that it also set the pattern for many other modern End Times groups. Its founder never sought to exploit or disadvantage anybody, but unfortunately his work has become an easy target for those who see only failure where hope was really the prevalent emotion.

There are always predictions of the end of the world, but some movements achieve more lasting fame than others. 1843 saw the Millerites awaiting the end, and anticipating the Messianic Age that would accompany it.

Up to 100,000 people actively believed in the predictions of William Miller, an uneducated farmer who had been studying the "chronological portions" of the apocalyptic passages of the Bible for many years. Like other scholars of "apocalyptic", Miller based his predictions on the Biblical books of Daniel and Revelation, supported by calculations from Ezekiel and Numbers. He depended for his specific calculations on two of the "dates" verses from Daniel, involving symbolic periods of 2,300 days, and 70 weeks. Unusually, he was reticent about the secret that he believed he had unravelled, worried that he would mislead people if he was wrong. Only in 1831, five years after completing his calculations, did he start delivering his findings as lectures or sermons. He found an immediately receptive audience.

Initially, Miller predicted the Second Coming in 1843, then later said it would occur between March 21, 1843 and March 21, 1844. He claimed no particular inspiration or authority for his findings, conducting himself on the basis that given sufficient application, others could have reached the same conclusion. He might not have achieved lasting fame but for Joshua V Himes, a Boston pastor, who had a remarkable knack for publicity and the use of modern communications. He founded major newspapers – the *Signs of the Times* in Boston, the *Philadelphia Alarm*, and the *Midnight Cry* in New York.

Himes also organised camp meetings at which Miller delivered his sequence of lectures, which were attended by thousands. The Millerites quickly became a substantial movement, although Miller apparently had no interest in being a charismatic leader. Movements can grow so easily where there is a need, and in New York State, where the movement was based, social and economic conditions were dire. Failures in agriculture, floods and epidemics, were followed by a national banking crisis, and the Signs of the Times were then, as they often seem to be, all too easy to read.

Increasingly, Miller's predictions were seen as specifically aimed at March 21, 1844, but when that day came and went, he recalculated the date as 22 October, 1844. The majority of his followers stood by him, terming the failure of prophecy the "First Disappointment". The popular press turned as unpleasant as it often does, and described Millerites behaving like fanatics, leaving homes and possessions, and dressing in robes for the occasion. In reality, they mostly gathered in their meeting halls where in due course they experienced "The Great Disappointment".

Although the press seriously exaggerated the effects of the prophecy's failure, a number of believers were admitted to asylums in the aftermath of the movement's collapse. Undaunted, many joined other popular "Adventist" groups. The Seventh-Day Adventists grew from the Millerite movement, and in time, one of the offshoot groups from the Adventist movement was that which David Koresh took to Waco, where he died with his followers in 1993.

Earth Lodge and Ghost Dance

If you want to find a perfect example of visions and prophecies growing out of suffering, upheaval and oppression, the Native people of the USA offer a sad lesson. The white settlers had brought disease and the evils of alcohol. The non-human intelligences who contacted the religious leaders of many of the tribes during the 1800s spoke sharply against strong drink, and mixing with the whites, and tried to stop the struggles and fights between the native tribes. Many promised protection for those who were faithful and behaved properly, protection from disease and injustice in some cases, and in others, like the Earth Lodge cult, from an imminent destruction brought by floods and earthquakes. The Earth Lodge actually built circular underground chambers where they would be able to shelter, with long access corridors where dance rituals could be performed. The prophet Wodziwob, from whose movement the Ghost Dance developed later, announced that dramatic earth changes would shake the whole world, and the earth would swallow up the white people, but leave their buildings, goods and tools for the native people to use. The Ghost Dance itself often involved belief in a legendary figure who would "bring back the dead as well as all animal life as soon as the grass was high in the fields." I think there can be no more attractive promise than the restoration of what we held dear and have recently lost. Sadly, we know that in this case the losses have never really ended.

Beliefs based on prophecies and promises of the end of suffering, the coming of justice, and the assurance of a safe, happy, and comfortable future have occurred for thousands of years, all over the world; they form an important part of dealing with the horrors of living with oppression or slavery. Where there are no prospects of improvement in the life you're leading, you look for prospects in another life. There are still parts of the world where the need for these beliefs exist, and I think they can usually be distinguished from the other forms of prophecy and expectation that I'm writing about. But I wouldn't always be sure of that. The murderous and destructive nature of many modern cults still, as we'll see, has the power to shock and astonish.

Chapter 5

THE NOSTRADAMUS PROBLEM

There is another kind of prophecy, that doesn't grow out of suffering and oppression, and isn't particularly concerned about the fate of individuals at the end of the world. There always have been prophets of events, people who simply claim to know what will happen in the future, and who pass their knowledge on to others. In the ancient world most of these prophets – oracles as they were often known – devoted their time to forecasting the likely success or failure of military actions, invasions, conquests. Or they dealt with the futures of rich and wealthy individuals, who wanted to know what greater wealth and power they would achieve, would they be king or queen, would they survive long enough to achieve their ambitions. For prophets of that kind, the end of the world was not a priority. The last thing that an ambitious member of a royal dynasty wanted to hear was that his world was going to end. Wise prophets didn't usually give bad news, or if they did they disguised it with great care. This may be why there are few End Times prophecies recorded from before the time of Christ.

The earlier predictions of Nostradamus were very much in the ancient tradition, given to the rich and famous for their own purposes, and concerned with affairs of state, war and succession. As time went on, his predictions became more wide-ranging, but also much more mysterious. We need to understand a little about the man to make any sense of his prophecies.

A Remarkable Man

Michel Nostradamus is the most famous prophet not to have become a vital part of a religious belief. Since his death in 1566 his fame has never dissipated, and more than 400 years later he commands a wider audience than ever. What makes the writings of a French doctor from so long ago seem so vital to the future of so many? Was he able to access information about the future? And do his prophecies really enable us to know what is going to happen in the next few years?

Were even half of what has been said about the life and background of Nostradamus true, he would undoubtedly be a remarkable man. And since at least half of it does seem to be true, he probably really was that remarkable. Because our mission here is with the future, I'll avoid most of the sequence of legends and half-truths that usually introduce accounts of his prophecies. But Nostradamus is a man worth knowing about.

His family was, by tradition, Jewish, although in the time of his grandfather, the same religious and social pressures that caused so many others to change the name of their faith saw his family becoming Christian, with the result that Michel was raised in Roman Catholicism. He was born in 1503, and had he professed any other faith in France at that time, he would never have achieved the respectability and fame that became his. He might have been lucky to survive so long.

Educated at St Remy till he was 16 years old, he then went to the highly-respected university at Montpellier, in Provence. He proved himself very able, and graduated in Medicine at twenty-two, receiving his license to practice four years later, still young for a trained doctor at that time. He married, and had children.

Among the detail that I will ignore, but you can find elsewhere, his commitment to working as a plague doctor stands out. This was one of the most dangerous and frustrating occupations open to a man of his skill and training, and he took his knowledge out into towns and villages where others were afraid to go. He had some success, too, with a reputedly higher survival rate among his patients than other doctors doing similar work. This may have been due to his commitment to standards of cleanliness and hygiene seldom adopted at that time. However, he could not save his own wife and some of his children with his treatments, and after their deaths he threw himself even harder into his work.

The progression from medicine to prophecy may seem an unlikely one, but in the 16th Century astrology was regarded as a science, and its study was part of medical training. The idea that higher influences shaped human lives ran consistently through religion, medicine and science. Predictions of future events were not the work of outcasts and unacceptables, or regarded as a sign of madness. If the predictions turned out to be correct, they were consistent with intellect and wisdom. If not, well, there are always excuses for failed prophecy.

Because this is a book about the future, about the next few years, I'll avoid the traditional look at the prophecies Nostradamus made relating to his own times. I don't think they've all been debunked, and I suspect that some of them were surprisingly accurate. How much this resulted from his great intelligence, and his understanding of the important people about whom he mostly prophesied we'll never know, but he did make a name for himself with all kinds of people.

The Method

Nostradamus's methods of obtaining information about the future are intriguing. Wherever I find an account of ritual, paraphernalia and odd pieces of equipment being used to produce perceptions that are almost certainly mental and internal, I suspect that the paraphernalia is just what the prophet, or magician or whatever, needs to have around to get into the mood for some communication with a non-human intelligence or two. Nostradamus describes his paraphernalia, and his mental attitude, in the opening quatrains of the first Century of his prophecies, here translated by James Randi:

Sitting by night in my secret study

Alone, resting upon the stool of brass

A slight flame, going out of the solitude,

Makes me pronounce what is not to be believed vain.

The wand in hand, set in the middle of the branches,

From the wave I wet both the hem and the foot,

In fear I write, trembling in the sleeves,

Divine splendour, the Divine seated nearby.

Randi points out the similarities to the ritual layout at the ancient Oracle at Delphi, and has found an account by Nostradamus of one particular ritual, apparently conducted over nine nights, that eventually resulted in his using some sort of automatic writing to obtain alchemical recipes. He produced some Latin verse, and then

"the back of my neck ornamented with branches of laurel, and my forehead bound with a crown of laurel and periwinkle, I beseeched my guardian angel in order to obtain these transmutations, to inspire me with truthful oracles, thanks to the intercession of Jesus Christ, the Virgin Mary and my invincible patron, the archangel Michael. He then appeared to me in a dream, and answered me in these terms..."

What this helpful archangel answered with seems to have been unimportant, but the mixture of influences here is fascinating. There are elements of pre-Christian paganism, rituals from ceremonial magic, alchemy as a representative of contemporary science, poetry, religious invocation, an angelic "guide" of the highest order, and a vision in a dream. It seems that having received his inspirations and written them down, Nostradamus would then attempt to use astrology to sort out dates and other details to identify, and place in time the events of which he had become aware.

A lot of prophecy

By these means, and maybe more besides, Nostradamus produced vast quantities of prophecy. Something like 950 different four-line quatrains, divided into 10 "Centuries", as well as countless other presages, letters and other documents. I don't suppose that all have survived, but many were widely published during his lifetime, and have been available to interpreters for more than 400 years. The early French versions are hard to find, but generally accurate representations of them are readily available, and several published interpretations of some or all of the prophecies are always in print. I'll refer to some of these interpreters by name – details of their books are given in the references for this chapter.

Before considering whether Nostradamus offers real, specific prophecies of the end of the world, let's get a feeling for the quatrains. Understanding the obscure French, bits of Latin, and complex sentence construction that he used is a daunting proposition. The Centuries will never be used for students to show their ability in translating from French to any other language. So many meanings can be, and have been, given to so many of the quatrains that it is clearly impossible to decide what is "right" and what is "wrong".

In the spirit of suggesting ways for you to investigate claims of prophecy, and draw your own conclusions, it's worth looking at one quatrain which, honestly, I picked at random. This is Quatrain 13, Century 2, and in the original French, probably just as Nostradamus himself wrote it down, it reads:

Le corps sans ame plus n'estre en sacrifice,

Jour de la mort mis en nativite,

L'esprit divin fera l'ame felice

Voyant le verbe et son eternite.

Those of you whose French is as bad as mine will be pleased to have a translation, but you don't have only the one. Henry C Roberts reads its meaning as:

The body without soul shall be no more admitted in sacrifice,

The day of death placed on the birthday,

The divine spirit shall make the soul happy,

By seeing the voice in its eternity.

Erika Cheetham, however, translates the same 26 French words as:

The body without a soul no longer at the sacrifice.

At the day of death it is brought to rebirth.

The divine spirit will make the soul rejoice

seeing the eternity of the world.

Personally, I can't see how any specific historical event could be recognised from either version. There's no date, no person, no place, and the two or three separate sections of each translation have no apparent link with each other. But, the interpreters of Nostradamus have no such limitations. Roberts asserts that the quatrain "correctly predicts the change in the language of the Mass from Latin to the vernacular by authorisation of the Second Vatican Council of 1964. Cheetham, that it explains the personal religious beliefs of its author, and refers to the very dubious proposition that he successfully predicted his own death. Why either interpreter draws their individual conclusions is never explained.

A quatrain recently interpreted as predicting the prevalence of the HIV virus, AIDS, and the other social and physical ills of our time – the "multi-plague" – is Quatrain 6 of Century II. The French says:

Aupres des portes et dedans deux citez

Seront deux fleaux onc n'apperceu un tel

Faim dedans peste, de fer hors gens boutez

Crier secours au grand Dieu immortel.

Which translates along the lines of:

Near the gates and between two cities

there will be two pestilences (or scourges) like none ever seen.

Famine, within plague, people thrust out by the sword,

crying for help to the great almighty God.

Despite some disagreement about the third line, the translation is similar among most interpreters. The meaning given to the words is a quite different matter. Cheetham and JH Brennan affirm that it refers to the dropping of atomic weapons at Hiroshima and Nagasaki in 1945. Jean Charles de Fontbrune that it refers to "The destruction of Paris and Geneva. The Exodus of their populations." Henry Roberts has no doubt that it "clearly predicts the Berlin Wall." Personally, I find it hard to choose. Any or all might fit, and so might none at all. As for Peter Lorie's judgment that it refers to a social epidemic, made up of the HIV virus, syphilis, poverty, depression, drug abuse, and ignorance and prejudice, I can think of nothing useful to say!

This is a straightforward example of what I've ended up regarding as the "Nostradamus Problem". The material the interpreters choose to work with is almost always so vague, so disjointed, so lacking in dates, names or places, that they can make of it what they will. I can do the same, and so can you. And because we all tend to do our interpreting in the light of events we know about personally, any one quatrain can be interpreted to give several different meanings, over a period of time. None is definitive, because the quatrains almost always defy exact interpretation. But almost any can be made attractive to an audience who want to know that Nostradamus successfully made prophecies about the particular times they live in. Those who thrill to future prophecy want a threat or promise that they can see come true. The vagueness of the quatrains is only a problem if you want to establish the truth. For those who write books of interpretation, it's a positive blessing.

1999, the King of Terror and the King of the Mongols

So, are there exceptions? Is there a single quatrain among nearly a thousand that we can be sure has not been given meaning before now? One that clearly refers to our future, to the next few years? Specifically to the year 2000, even? I expect that you've heard that Nostradamus has predicted the when and how of the end of the world. Where and how does he do it?

Well, there is Quatrain 77 of Century 8, which clearly refers to a "Third Antichrist", and a war for which he is responsible that lasts for twenty-seven years. And there's Quatrain 74 of Century 10, which Stewart Robb in particular interprets as the dead rising from their tombs "not far from the great age thousand". But bear in mind that Nostradamus wrote in the context of what was Biblically correct at his time, and that included the inevitability, because it was clearly written in the Bible, of a sequence of Antichrists. There are no names, or dates here, and I suggest that Nostradamus never knew who any Antichrist might be, or when or where he (or she?) might turn up. I think that he was being careful not to offend the religious authorities, while still providing interesting reading for his public. There had to be an Antichrist or three, so he fitted them in where he could.

Antichrists aside, there is really only one rock-solid, end of this Millennium quatrain. The salvation of the interpreters, the holy grail of those excited by the prospect of imminent doom. You'll find it highlighted in almost every book about Nostradamus, and you'll hear a lot about it in the next three or four years. And because it actually includes a date that doesn't depend on astrological calculation, or cracking some obscure code it has never, to my knowledge, been interpreted as referring to any other event. It's Quatrain 72 of Century 10, and in French it reads:

"L'an mil neuf cens nonante neuf sept mois

Du ciel viendra grand Roy deffraieur

Reusciter le grand Roy d'Angolmois.

Auant apres Mars regner par bon heur."

You won't be surprised to know that the second, third and fourth lines are open to speculation. They sound as if they contain some pretty frightening stuff, and we'll look at them closely. But to start with, that first line, simply translated, means:

"The year 1999 and seven months"

Which is specific. There's just a handful of real dates in the Centuries, and this is the only date between now and a vague one about five hundred years ahead. So, in July or, given the change in calendars maybe August of 1999, what's going to happen? We can take the first line as read, and weigh up what the interpreters make of the rest.

Roberts translates: "From the skies shall come an alarmingly powerful king, to raise again the great King of Jacquerie. Before and after, Mars shall reign at will." He says that: "A tremendous world revolution is foretold to take place in the year 1999, with a complete upheaval of existing social orders, preceded by world-wide wars." Of the mysterious "Roy d'Angolmois, he concludes that this is an anagram for "Roi de Mongulois" (King of the Mongolians). "The threat of war will come from the east. Eastern Russia? Tibet? China? Mongolia?"

In Fontbrune 1, the quatrain is headed, "The Airborne Invasion of France in July 1999", and the interpretation tells us that, "a great, terrifying leader will come through the skies to revive (the memory of) the great conqueror of Angouleme. Before and after war will rule luckily." We are reminded of the locusts in the Book of Revelation also coming "through the skies", and that, "The people of Angouleme (Angoulmois) were conquered by the Visigoths and soon invaded by the Huns, a

Mongol race under the command of Attila."

Erika Cheetham settles for: "from the sky will come the great King of Terror. He will bring back to life the great king of the Mongols. Before and after War reigns happily." Then she goes straight for the target: "Nostradamus seems to foresee the end of the world at the Millennium, the year 2000... first we must suffer the Asian antichrist 'the King of Mongols'."

Brennan takes an unusual line with the "great King of Terror". Remarking that whoever is able to resuscitate the King of the Mongols – Genghis Khan, dead since 1227 – must be remarkable, he speculates along a new line. "Is it possible we are back to the extra-terrestrial hypothesis, with national and international differences abruptly dwarfed by the appearance of a terrifying, but technically advanced, alien life form capable of cloning the cells of our ancient dead to produce a spurious resurrection?"

James Randi, arch-sceptic in most things, but the author of a well informed book about Nostradamus, has a simple commentary on this most vital of quatrains. "Ho hum," he says. He's as likely to be right as anybody.

A century too far?

So, that's the only quatrain that is undeniably connected with dramatic changes over the next few years, around the millennium. You can find quatrains that some interpreters back as being relevant, but that others ignore, or understand to mean something entirely different. How can we start making informed decisions about how likely Nostradamus is to be right about "1999 and seven months". If he was a horse, would you consider putting money on him? What sort of return would you expect on your investment?. Maybe we can learn something by looking at how Nostradamus has fared in predicting other disasters and conflagrations in this century. Was he really able to receive information about what would happen so far in the future?

Two World Wars

A few years ago I was writing some articles about the "No-War Prophecies" made before the Second World War. The publisher asked me if I could research the subject further, and find out whether there were any convincing prophecies of either of the World Wars, 1914-

1918, or 1939-1945. Not prophecies that were interpreted and under-stood after the wars had begun, but that were sufficiently clear to enable predictions to be made before the event.

I immediately thought of Nostradamus. If one theme is constant throughout the Centuries, it is his commitment to France. To the Royal Family in particular, but also to its fortunes in battle, its welfare, the safety of its people. And if any one country was at the centre of the two world wars this century, it was France. It was a battleground for the rest of Europe, and the country and its people suffered appallingly. If he was receiving impressions of vivid and important events that were to come in the future of his country, there were so many that could have been received about the First and Second World Wars. Not just techno-logical achievements that may have been beyond his comprehension, like radar, but vivid events involving endless land battles, the trenches, tanks, the arrival of Hitler in Paris, the formation and role of the Vichy Government, the Resistance and the deportation and death of many Jews, his own people.

So I delved into a range of sources. A particularly useful one was a report called "War Prophecies", published by the Society for Psychical Research in 1916. Looking for prophecies with any relevance at all was clearly a frustrating task for the author. There were some arithmetical coincidences in the life of the first German Emperor, which saw the end of the German Empire in 1913. There was the falsely dated "Prophecy of Lehnin", which had the last German emperor being murdered by a Jew. There was the Prophecy of Mayence, a vague prediction of European war, which had already been applied to events in 1849 and 1850, but had recently been revived. There was Mme de Thebes, who in the early years of the century had predicted European war in 1913, among numerous other events that never happened at all. Old Moore's Almanack for 1914 failed to mention the war. Unfortunately, so did the issue for 1915, which had gone to print before July 1914!

Nostradamus doesn't get a mention in the SPR report, although it wasn't long since the translation of many of the quatrains by Charles Ward, and many of the bright and able members of the Society would have been aware of the prophecies. Nowhere could I find any inter-pretation of Nostradamus predicting the First World War, by events, dates, names of personalities, or in any other way. Yes, you can find plenty of detailed interpretations made after the events had taken place, but not one from before hostilities began.

When it came to looking at the Second World War, which ravaged France socially and physically from 1939 to 1945, I had no more success. Worse, in fact, because when I recently tracked down some of the more obscure interpretations of Nostradamus published during the war, I found that even then, intelligent and committed interpreters could find nothing substantial to say about how the war would end, and were actually less than sure about which side would win.

In 1941 Stewart Robb, an Oxford MA, published *Nostradamus on Napoleon, Hitler and the Present Crisis*. Robb may have been the first to produce the "Hister/Hitler" link, although he acknowledged that Hister was the Latin name for the River Danube, and that making "Hitler" into "Hister" took some doing, even by the liberal rules for writing anagrams that were current when Nostradamus was writing. Incidentally, why Nostradamus should have felt it necessary to make an anagram of the name of the man who did more damage to France than anyone else in modern times is a mystery to me. As an excuse for the obscurity of the language of the quatrains, we are told that Nostradamus changed and confused the text of the quatrains because he feared the Inquisition, and accusations of witchcraft. We are also told that he knew the date of his own death. I wonder why he feared to identify a man whom the world wouldn't hear of for 300 years, when he would be long since dead?

Stewart Robb made some exotic interpretations of quatrains he felt reflected the war to date, and then tried a handful of unsuccessful predictions under the heading, "The Shape of Things to Come". I don't recall reading that "Franco met Mussolini on the Riviera, and refused to cooperate with the Axis to let troops pass through Spain to Gibraltar", or that General De Gaulle entered Rome after the war, "leading a great band of banished and exiled." A bloody invasion of Italy by "a world conqueror from Arabia" seems unlikely. The concentration camps, the Holocaust, the horrors suffered by both armies in Russia, even the dropping of the atomic bomb, just don't rate a mention.

HI Woolf, writing in 1944, fared little better. The Duke of Windsor did not face a horrible death while riding on horseback, being dragged along the ground with his foot caught in a stirrup. Churchill, Roosevelt and Stalin never moved the Vatican from Italy. All things considered, I strongly suspect that whatever Nostradamus may have known about events during his own lifetime, he had no information at all about either World War. There is simply no evidence to suggest that he did.

The Kennedy Myth

Most major world events attract the attention of the interpreters, and the Kennedy assassinations in 1963 and 1968 provided an ideal opportunity. The singer Al Stewart included the Kennedys in his epic song "Nostradamus" in 1973:

"In the new lands of America three brothers now shall come to power

Two alone are born to rule, but all shall die before their hour."

Sadly for the interpreters, but maybe happily for Ted Kennedy, there is nothing that specific in the quatrains. Quatrain 26 of Century One, which Cheetham and Brennan interpret as referring to the two assassinations, says something like, to use Cheetham's version:

"The great man will be struck down in the day by a thunderbolt.

An evil deed, foretold by the bearer of a petition.

According to the prediction another falls at night time."

The same quatrain was seen differently by Henry Roberts writing in 1949. He decided that it referred to:

"the taking over of Czechoslovakia by Hitler, the resignation of President Benes, the dissensions over the matter between France and England, and the dire warning of the consequences of this betrayal, [all are] remarkably outlined in this prophecy."

Other "Kennedy" references can supposedly be found in Quatrains 46 and 77 of Century 8. Using Cheetham's words again, 46 says that, "When Mars will take up his horrible throne, the Cock and the Eagle, France and the three brothers". 77 is translated as, "The antichrist very soon annihilates the three."

The name "Kennedy" never appears in the quatrains. There are no dates or places relating to any of the brothers. And Ted Kennedy has lived on to complete a successful political career. The Kennedy tragedies were the sort that people like to think have been predicted, perhaps because it gives their deaths some sort of meaning, and makes random, destructive killings seem somehow less wasteful than they really were. But in the case of Nostradamus, there isn't any genuine solace to be found.

An Outstanding Failure?

In the blurb for his more recent book, *Nostradamus – The Millennium and Beyond*, author Peter Lorie refers to his being "co-author of the previous world-wide million copy bestseller, *Nostradamus – The End of the Millennium*". The earlier book had presented "Prophecies 1992 to 2001", many of which remain to be fulfilled – or not. Co-author VJ Hewitt had, apparently, "spent more than a decade developing a precise numerical decoding system that she has applied to the famous quatrains from Nostradamus's "The Centuries". This extraordinary code, when applied, permits an accuracy that has never before been achieved, providing us with precise dates and locations out of the sometimes confusing texts." While the interpretations dealing with events that had occurred before the book was written are quite accurate, the code is so radical, effectively rewriting quatrains from beginning to end by using a "meltdown process producing another anagram", that I cannot hold Nostradamus in any way responsible for what became Hewitt's own prophecies. Unfortunately, these included:

"Charles, Prince of Wales, marries his frivolous Diana Spencer at the temple of St Paul. She will become a queen who joins her pensive king in reviving a fleeting monarchy.

"During 1995, Switzerland's financial reputation and consequently her wealth are destroyed, with the revelation of this secret fraud operating from 1991.

"Although George Bush is re-elected President in 1992, his running mate this time is not Vice-President Dan Quayle.

"After 4th January 1992 the Roman Catholic Church will no longer be able to disguise the numbers of their priests who are both HIV positive and already developing the AIDS disease... As a result, from 1st February 1995 many priests are not only socially ruined, but imprisoned.

"Beginning in 1992 and ending in 1993, the coronation of King Charles and the Olympic Games will be followed by a great earthquake, triggered off by a shifting in the San Andreas fault... A mass evacuation begins from cities and towns before the earthquake. The State Governor organises the exodus to the border where it stays outside the ring, the shadow, the zone... San Diego disappears beneath the sea... Hollywood film studios collapse... America burns 1993-1996.

"The date 6th March 1995 may be the time of her (Margaret Thatcher's) re-election to leadership of the party. However, there is the hint that she may only become leader of the opposition, as perhaps the Conservatives are no longer in power."

I rest my case. Prophecy doesn't come much worse than this but, good or absolutely rotten, there's a reading public out there which clearly wants prophecy, regardless of its quality. If a million people choose to buy a book, then who am I to criticise? Envy isn't a desirable characteristic in an author.

Utter fabrication?

During the Second World War, both British and Germans thought it worth making some slight adaptations to Nostradamus for propaganda purposes. The Germans, not surprisingly, published speculative interpretations of existing quatrains which suggested victory for their side, and social panic and disorder in Great Britain. The British, apparently, utilised the talents of one Louis de Wohl, a refugee from Germany who said that he knew Hitler's astrologer. As well as writing "fake astrological articles for equally fake astrological magazines that contained discouraging predictions for Nazi Germany", he also devised a book of Nostradamian prophecies – some fictional, some doctored – which was dropped in quantity from planes over Germany in 1943. The power and attraction of Nostradamus somehow never abates.

Simpler than adapting or reinterpreting genuine quatrains is inventing entirely new ones, and implying genuine authorship. It was done during the years following the death of Nostradamus, and it has been done since. In 1983 and 1991, with some slight adaptations in-between, editions appeared of the mysteriously authored, rather slim volume *Nostradamus' Unpublished Prophecies*, the more recent version also "Including Persian Gulf Update".

I'd like to share with you some of the reported background to these "unpublished prophecies":

"A curious manuscript has been making the rounds of Europe... The legend goes that shortly before his death, Nostradamus penned a series of prophecies so startling that he never had them included in any of his published works, too afraid was he of the effect they may have. These predictions were circulated only to royalty and were thought destroyed for many years until they were uncovered in the basement of the house where Nostradamus died. They were sealed behind a wall which only recently was torn down to reinforce the old building which is now a landmark... as far as we can tell, there are 51 pages in the previously uncovered manuscript. However, many of the words and entire sentences are said to be so faded from age that they could not be easily translated."

The unnamed author of this work appears to be the only person who has heard of the manuscript or, indeed, knew about the wall of the house being torn down. Another mystery is that there is no French version of any of these additional prophecies. But they are, fortunately, remarkably precise. About the return of Jesus Christ:

"In the millennium, two, the King's Son, before the turn
Is seen by all amid thunderclaps.
Angry, the rubble of war and pestilence, the sins,
The fish returns to power after a long sleep.
About a new life on earth under Christ's care:
A new leader from the heavens brings the people
Together as one, all factions die and are reborn.
Exalted clergy bends to a higher rule. Angels are
Seen in joy. The Red Man dissolves in a bottomless pit."

And about the USA, Russia and China joining in a pact against alien invasion:

"A salver flies, comes to rest in the New City.
Hate flourishes for the entity within. Battle lines
Drawn. Fears of disease mask truth while three
Leaders in secret, unite against a false threat."

If nothing else, these "unpublished quatrains" prove that anybody can write a Nostradamian prophecy – even if they don't know any French!

Finally, perhaps the most ambitious, or audacious, of all the interpreters of Nostradamus is the American author Dolores Cannon, who claims to be recording the channelled communications of the long-dead prophets. So far, Cannon has produced three substantial books of this extraordinary material. These include two different sources of new prophecy, as Nostradamus corrects the interpretation of the quatrains he wrote while alive, and provides hundreds of new ones! Why he still has to frame "his" prophecies in rather poor, obscure four-line poems is a question that doesn't seem to have been asked, although his need to write in French appears to have passed. Couldn't he simply tell Ms

Cannon what is going to happen, and when, without any of the poetic nonsense, or wrapping the knowledge up in obscure symbols?

Real Prophecy?

So, was Nostradamus a late mediæval Doctor Who, uniquely free to experience future times and the events they would bring, able to see and hear but, sadly, seldom able to understand what he saw and heard? Was the failure in the magical link he established between the present and the future, or in his inability to comprehend and record what he saw, however clearly it may have been presented to him. If the perceptions were visual, surely a highly educated doctor, even with the observational and descriptive skills of the 16th Century, could have described pilots in oxygen masks better than as "pig-men"? A sputnik better than a "long-running spark"? If they were based on a knowledge of written words that described what would happen in the future, why make obscure anagrams of straightforward French names like Napoleon, or confuse Hitler with the River Danube?

I don't hold Nostradamus responsible for what has been done in his name. Interpreting his prophetic writing has often proved to be an easy way to make money. Interpreters take the obscure, confusing and archaic language of the quatrains, and they can find whatever they want. Many, most even, are absolutely convinced that their interpretations are correct, and significant, and worth sharing with the world. But those interpretations rarely survive serious analysis.

I'm not surprised that the mystique of Nostradamus as a unique prophet, with extraordinary knowledge of future events, is carefully preserved by those who produce interpretations of his words. They claim that Nostradamus is the real prophet, and they are simply interpreting his work. But the quatrains are so vague that he actually ceases to be the prophet, and the interpreters take his place. In considering the interpretations of Laver, Robb, Woolf, Cheetham, Fontbrune, Brennan, Hewitt, Lorie, Hogue and all the others, we are considering prophecies written not by Nostradamus himself, but by all those different individuals. A variety of prophets for their times, consistently unsuccessful where they dare to actually predict, rather than just look back.

There is now no way of knowing for certain what Nostradamus knew about the future, or felt, heard, saw or otherwise experienced. I think that he believed himself to be a genuine prophet, with a knowledge of future events obtained by essentially occult means which convinced important people of his abilities during his own lifetime. There were many who accepted and recognised his skills as remarkable. I can't prove that he didn't have some anomalous knowledge, and in view of more recent evidence of prescience and premonition of future events I retain an open mind.

So far as events in this century are concerned, the quatrains of Nostradamus seem to amount to no more than a verbal construction set; a big box of words, phrases and intimations which can be, and have been, assembled at will into a multitude of shapes and meanings. There is no evidence to suggest that Nostradamus had the least idea about the twentieth century, and I have yet to see a single quatrain that has been accurately interpreted before a single specific event in the past 96 years. Maybe I have high expectations, maybe I'm just too fussy, but what's the point of a prophecy that can't be understood till after the event it prophesies? Come July or August 1999, I'll be watching and waiting. But Nostradamus alone, nor his army of interpreters, won't have me on the edge of my seat.

Chapter 6

MESSAGES FROM MARY

Saints, angels and archangels make regular visits to Earth, appear in visions and give messages. Over the past decade a remarkable industry has grown up based around encounters with angels. It is as though the Almighty had suddenly discovered the principles of customer service, or total quality management, or something. As if He has restructured the role of the Angelic Host, telling them to get out there and mix, meet people face to face, be ready to intervene in potential accidents and disasters much as Superman would. To stand in for the Samaritans in counselling and crisis intervention. Even, it seems, to take on the matchmaking role from Cupid. You can phone premium rate phone numbers to obtain angelic advice. It was never like that in the good old days, when angels only became involved in human affairs on the most vital and significant issues, like announcing miraculous pregnancies and births, or appearing to figures of world importance.

Recent trends aside, in Roman Catholic tradition there has always been one person who has the duty of contact and communication between Earth and Heaven. This is the Blessed Virgin Mary, the mother of Jesus Christ. Hers remains the single most frequent vision seen around the world.

The tradition of visions of the Virgin Mary is a long one, and the earliest reports of visionary experiences date back to about 300 AD. Here in England, the earliest substantial report comes from the Norfolk town of Walsingham, where the lady of the manor, Richeldis, was visited three times during the 11th century. She saw an image of the house at Nazareth where Christ had grown up, and was told to build a copy of that house on her own land at Walsingham. This she did, and Walsingham is still a major centre of pilgrimage.

There are several European reports from the Middle Ages, and the appearance of Our Lady of Guadalupe, in Mexico in 1531, led to an image of the vision apparently appearing on the tilma – a long outer cape – belonging to the witness. This continues to be an important object of devotion.

The modern pattern of visions was largely set when, in 1830, a devoted young Catholic nun, Catherine Laboure, was told by the Virgin Mary to have a religious medal made in the form of the vision she had seen. The image on this "Miraculous Medal", since distributed all round the world, may well have suggested to later visionaries the figure that they would see. And the vision had spoken to the witness. From then on the visions usually would.

La Salette – prophecy and more prophecy

In 1846, the first major reported vision involving young children took place. Melanie Mathieu, 15, and Maximin Giraud, 11, were out looking after cattle in the country near Grenoble when they fell asleep. The cows had, it seems, moved on, the children went to look for them, and as Melanie recalled it shortly after the event:

"When I was five or six steps off the little stream, I saw a brightness like the sun, it was far more brilliant, but it had not the same colour. And I said to Maximin, 'Come quick and see the bright light down there' and Maximin came down saying, 'Where is it?' I pointed to it near the little spring, and he stopped when he saw it. Then we saw a lady in the bright light; she was sitting with her head in her hands... then the lady rose up, crossed her arms, and said to us, "Come near, my children, be not afraid. I am here to tell you great news."

And she told them some remarkable things, changing after a while from the French language, which the children didn't understand well, to the local Bigourdan dialect. She talked – as so many visionary figures have since – about the decline in social behaviour, about the Sabbath not being observed, about cart-drivers swearing. She spoke of the disease in the local potato harvest, saying that it was a result of the local people's behaviour. She prophesied about the potatoes that: "They will continue to decay, so that by Christmas there will be none left." It seems that by December 1846, potatoes could not be bought in the area.

Other predictions were made, although with the proviso that if people behaved in accordance with the vision's instructions, the promised misery could be avoided. The children's accounts seem to have been consistent with each other over a number of interviews and interrogations. They reported that the vision had said, "There will come a great famine. Before the famine comes, the children under seven years of age will be seized with trembling, and will die in the hands of those that hold them. The walnuts will become bad, the grapes will rot."

After giving more warnings that mankind should change its ways, Melanie said, "the beautiful lady arose a little from the ground, then she looked towards heaven, then towards the earth; then we saw her head no more, then her arms no more, then her feet no more; we saw nothing more than a brightness in the air; after this the brightness disappeared. Afterwards we looked after our cows."

Not long after the vision had taken place, when the children's reports of the event were already well known, the disease phylloxera struck the grape crop. A form of cholera affecting only young children reached epidemic proportions, causing two hours of shaking and sickness before almost certain death. The walnut crop failed. Apparently, the unacceptable behaviour had not sufficiently improved, and the threats included in the vision's predictions had become realities. Because of what I understand to be true about La Salette, and the success of the prophecies there, I never dismiss the possibility of a vision providing genuine knowledge of future events.

A yet more remarkable element of the La Salette story actually came to light in 1878, 32 years after the vision. For reasons we'll never be able to know, Melanie set a pattern repeated again and again in the world of visions and prophecies. After 30 years or so in various convents and religious houses, she wrote down a new account of the vision she had experienced as an uneducated teenager, and this new account contained her recollections of messages that she had never before recalled in public. Or perhaps never really recalled at all. As has happened some time after more recent visions, the new recollections were substantially prophetic.

None of these prophecies appeared in a thorough investigation of the original vision published in English in 1854, written by the Archbishop of Birmingham. But they are intriguing. Melanie recalled that the Virgin had given specific predictions relating to the years 1859, 1864 and 1865, none of which appeared to have really come about. Of more interest to us are the graphic, if undated end times prophecies:

"There will be a series of wars until the last war, which will then be fought by the ten kings of the Antichrist, all of whom will have one and the same plan and will be the only rulers of the world... the Antichrist will be born of a Hebrew nun, a false virgin who will communicate with the old serpent, the master of impurity, his father will be a bishop... he will have brothers who, although not devils incarnate like him, will be children of evil... The seasons will be altered, the earth will produce nothing but bad fruit, the stars will lose their regular motions, the moon will reflect only a faint reddish glow. Water and fire will give the Earth's globe convulsions and terrible earthquakes which will swallow up mountains and cities... Rome will lose the faith and become the seat of the Antichrist."

And so it goes on, moving into the traditional Second Coming sequence of events. Yet these prophecies intrigue me. It isn't that they've come true – I'm happy to say – but they do contain some key elements that appear in later prophecies. There's definite suggestions of the New World Order, of the modern view of the Antichrist as an apparent worker of good works, and unifier of nations. There's the "ten kings" – reminiscent of later theories about the Common Market. And there's the "environmental" material. I've only included a few short sections of the much longer account given by Melanie, an account that is seldom published or referred to outside conservative Catholic circles. Given the background of apparent success, we should keep this one in mind. If the accounts of events were accurate, either the Virgin Mary, or Melanie herself, showed a definite aptitude for knowing the future.

The famous visions at Lourdes, where the Virgin Mary appeared to Bernadette Soubirous in 1858, involved little significant conversation, and no real prophecy. The next major vision was at Pontmain, in France, in 1871. Here, during the Franco-Prussian War four young children watched a silent and very elegant vision which included the appearance of encouraging words on a sort of scroll under the figure of Mary. If any future was predicted, it was a very immediate one. It is said that at the moment the vision began, the nearby German troops unexpectedly halted their advance into France. Legend has it that the Prussian commander said next morning, "We cannot go farther. Yonder, in the direction of Brittany, there is an invisible Madonna barring the way."

Visions continued to occur frequently, always witnessed by individuals with a knowledge of the Catholic faith, often by children or adolescents. In 1917 the visions at Fatima, Portugal, took place, and a most extraordinary story of End Times fears, hopes and prophecies began.

Rather like the delayed recollections of Melanie at La Salette, the story of the messages received by three young children at the Cova de Iria, near Fatima, is a very confusing one. You wouldn't necessarily know just how confusing it is from reading the many modern books on the subject. A jigsaw of strange information, probably with pieces missing, has been smoothed over to look like a coherent and very beautiful picture. But I've been researching this part of the Fatima story for 15 years now, and there's probably as many years of work yet to go. I don't have space to tell the full story of the visions themselves, or even attempt to explain the legendary "Dance of the Sun" – for which I have no satisfactory explanation. But here's an update on the messages that weigh most heavily in the thinking of the Catholic church across the world, which are said by many to guide and inspire Pope John Paul II.

The Fatima Visions

The witnesses of the Fatima visions were three young and, almost inevitably where they lived, uneducated children. In 1917 when most – or maybe all – of the visions took place, the youngest child was seven, the next nine and the eldest, Lucia, was 10. The younger children died in the influenza epidemic after the First World War. Lucia is still alive as I write, having spent almost all of her life in various convents.

It isn't clear what each child saw and heard. I suspect that Francisco, the youngest, more or less recounted to investigators only what Lucia told him she had seen. It certainly appears that he never heard the Virgin Mary speak, and I doubt that Jacinta, the younger girl, really had a clear perception of the events reported by Lucia. Because of the early deaths of the younger children, it has been left to Lucia to clarify, rewrite and expand on the events of 1917, and of several other years, too. She has done this with some vigour, and it is now hard to tell what happened and when, what she was or wasn't told in 1917 or other visions, and whether we should accept it as genuine prophecy.

The visions of 1917 eventually attracted large numbers of hopeful pilgrims. At the final vision with the three children present, 50,000 – 80,000 people gathered in the Cova, drawn by the possibility of healing, the chance of sharing the children's visions, and the promise of a dramatic miracle. The last of these hopes may really have been fulfilled. That aside, the local priest, many visitors, and anti-religious local officials all took a great interest in the experiences reported by the children. They were thoroughly interviewed, asked what had happened, and what messages the vision had given. Their replies were written down at the time, but they are not at all consistent with what has been published since.

It wasn't surprising that the children reported that the vision had told them a secret. The children at La Salette had one, and once established, the pattern of events in visions has remained fairly constant. But in the interviews with the children at the time, there was only ever one secret. And it wasn't regarded as particularly important. Lucia was interviewed on September 13, 1917, and asked whether the secret had been told only to her, replied, "To all three of us." But after the final vision on October 13, 1917, Lucia wasn't sure whether or not the vision had told her the secret at the vision in July. When Francisco was asked on the same day whether the Lady, as she was referred to, had told him the secret, he replied, "It wasn't she; it was Lucia." Asked: "Is the secret good for your soul and Lucia's and Jacinta's souls?" he agreed that it was.

We know for certain of one serious failure in prophecy by the Lady. As Lucia was being carried among the huge crowd in the Cova after the final vision, and the "Dance of the Sun", she announced publicly that the war was about to end, and that the Portuguese soldiers would be coming home soon. Later that day she said that the vision had told her, "The war ends even today, wait here for the very brave soldiers." Jacinta confirmed this report. Sadly, the war dragged on for more than a year before the Armistice.

So, how did the Fatima Prophecies develop from the "one secret" of the contemporary interviews, a secret that was good for the souls of all three children, to a group of three separate secret prophecies, the last and greatest of which has become legend as the "Third Secret of Fatima"? The story behind the Third Secret will remind you of others from the world of prophecy. It was even the theme of the first *X-Files* comic book.

The Third Prophecy of Fatima?

After the deaths of Jacinta and Francisco, only Lucia was left alive to tell the story of what the three children had witnessed and experienced. Sights like small clouds, lights, and mysterious motion in the branches of the holm oak in the branches of which the Virgin had chosen, for some reason, to appear, were reported by a handful of people. But there was never any report by any member of the public of seeing the religious figures that Lucia and, to a lesser extent, the other children, said that they not only saw but heard. Remarkably, it seems that the three children did not even see the "Dance of the Sun", which raises

LE PETIT JOURNAL

ILLUSTRÉ

HEBDOMADAIRE · 36e Année
61, rue Lafayette, Paris

22 Novembre 1925 · N° 1822
PRIX : 30 CENTIMES

ASSISTERONS-NOUS A LA DESTRUCTION DE PARIS EN 1926 ?

Lire dans ce numéro les prédictions sensationnelles du célèbre fakir FHAKYA-KHAN

The end of the world… In 1925
the seer Fhakya-Khan predicted
that a fearsome cataclysm would
destroy Paris in the following year.
He was wrong, but his vision of
how the destruction would occur
reflects the views of many
prophets of doom.

Many millennial visions have been shaped by the influential Book of Revelation, which predicts huge locust-cum-horse-cum-scorpion beings sent to torment those left 'unsealed' by God.

Mother Shipton, the Yorkshire prophetess, was born in 1488. Her alleged prediction that "The world to an end shall come in eighteen hundred and eighty-one" was actually invented around 1850.

William Miller, one of the greatest of Christian millenarians, was the father of the Seventh-Day Adventist movement. Up to 100,000 followers waited for the Second Coming to occur as he had predicted in 1844.

The Second Coming of Christ, as predicted by William Miller. Basing his work on the Books of Ezekiel, Numbers, Daniel and Revelation, Miller arrived at a date between 21 March 1843 and 21 March 1844.

MICHEL NOSTRADAMUS.
Médecin,
Né à S.ᵗ Remy, en Provence, le 14 Décemb. 1503.
Mort le 2 juillet 1566.

Paris chez Odieuvre M.ᵈ d'Estampes, rue d'Anjou la derniere P.Cochere à gauche entrant par la rue Dauphine. C.P.R.

Nostradamus, the best-known prophet never to become the centre of a great religion, predicted that an apocalypse will occur in July 1999. Interpreters of his coded predictions have suggested the catalyst will be a great leader from central Asia who will unleash a terrible war on the rest of the world.

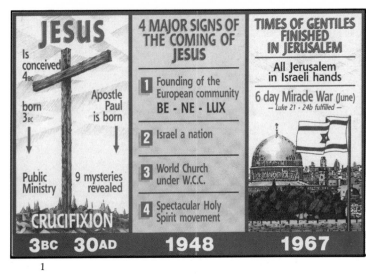

1

JESUS

Is conceived 4BC

born 3BC

Apostle Paul is born

Public Ministry

9 mysteries revealed

CRUCIFIXION

3BC 30AD

4 MAJOR SIGNS OF THE COMING OF JESUS

1 Founding of the European community **BE - NE - LUX**

2 Israel a nation

3 World Church under W.C.C.

4 Spectacular Holy Spirit movement

1948

TIMES OF GENTILES FINISHED IN JERUSALEM

All Jerusalem in Israeli hands

6 day Miracle War (June)
— Luke 21 - 24b fulfilled —

1967

2

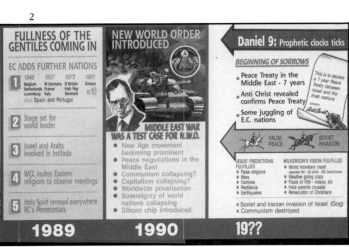

FULLNESS OF THE GENTILES COMING IN

EC ADDS FURTHER NATIONS

1

1948	1957	1973	1981
Belgium	W Germany	G Britain	Greece
Netherlands	France	Irish Rep	
Luxemburg	Italy	Denmark	=10

plus Spain and Portugal

2 Stage set for world leader

3 Israel and Arabs involved in Intifada

4 WCC invites Eastern religions to observe meetings

5 Holy Spirit renewal everywhere RC's-Pentecostals

1989

NEW WORLD ORDER INTRODUCED

MIDDLE EAST WAR WAS A TEST CASE FOR N.W.O.

- New Age movement becoming prominent
- Peace negotiations in the Middle East
- Communism collapsing?
- Capitalism collapsing?
- Worldwide privatization
- Sovereignty of world nations collapsing
- Silicon chip introduced.

1990

Daniel 9: Prophetic clocks ticks

BEGINNING OF SORROWS

- Peace Treaty in the Middle East - 7 years
- Anti Christ revealed confirms Peace Treaty
- Some juggling of E.C. nations

This is to declare a 7 year Peace Treaty between Israel and the Arab nations

FALSE PEACE   SOVIET INVASION

JESUS' PREDICTIONS FULFILLED	WILKERSON'S VISION FULFILLED
• False religions	• World monetary crash
• Wars	Japanese Yen - US dollar - WG Deutschmark
• Famines	• Weather going crazy
• Pestilence	• Flood of filth - videos, etc
• Earthquakes	• Hate parents crusade
	• Persecution of Christians

- Soviet and Iranian invasion of Israel (Gog)
- Communism destroyed

19??

The New Zealand evangelist Barry R Smith uses this metre-long diagram to sketch out the events leading up to the End Times: the time of Sorrows, Tribulation, Reign of Christ and the Battle of Armageddon, in which Christ will defeat the combined forces of Satan, the Pope and the President of the EEC.

Lucia, a peasant girl who was the principal witness to a series of visions of the Virgin Mary at Fatima in Portugal in 1917, later revealed that three great secrets had been confided to her. Two she published in 1941; the third was sealed and passed to the Vatican, where Pope John XXIII is thought to have opened it in 1959.

Edgar Cayce predicted the destruction of Japan and large parts of California before general devastation wrought by a shift in polar alignments around the year 2001. His other prophecies include the rediscovery of Atlantis and the rise of Livingston, Montana, to become the financial capital of the world.

David Koresh, the leader of the Branch Davidians, an offshoot of the millennial Adventist churches, believed he was the 'Lamb' of Revelation, fated to set in motion the events of the Biblical end times.

Texe Marrs, an American evange-list, predicts 'a brutal worldwide campaign of tyranny, deception, mass murder and dictatorial con-trol', orchestrated by the Green Party and President Clinton, will be in place by the year 2000.

Maria Devos led a religious cult, the White
Brotherhood, based in the Ukraine. Followers were
told she was the earthly incarnation of God and
would be crucified in Kiev on 11 November 1993. At
the same time 144,000 cult members would commit
suicide, only to be resurrected with Maria three days
later. In the event, the Brotherhood attracted only
1,000 devotees and the crucifixion never happened.

Predictions of doom continue to be made
as we approach the fateful year 2000.

serious question about the objectivity of that event. Lucia, however, has dramatically changed the historical record about Fatima, all from inside her convent walls.

We have, recently, become used to stories of strange events that appear to be told backwards – from the end, working back towards the beginning. This is particularly true of many "alien abduction" cases, which all too often start off looking like a straightforward sighting of a strange light or flying object, and end up with the "witness" recalling all sorts of extraordinary encounters, frequently during their childhood, sometimes even before birth. Lucia added visions in 1915 and 1916, before the major series in 1917, recounted several further visions after 1917, and came up with a far more complicated set of secrets and prophecies than ever seemed apparent when the children were inter-viewed in 1917.

As ever, I cannot say for certain that these additional events did not, in some sense, happen to Lucia. But I do have my doubts. Some of her reports appear to contradict the accounts of contemporary interviews, and the pattern of their development seems, now, so predictable. But they were a source of wonder to many when they started to be pub-lished early in the Second World War.

Lucia said that in 1915, the three children (then very young) sup-posedly had two experiences of a "figure poised in the air above the trees", which "looked like a statue made of snow", and like "a person wrapped up in a sheet". In 1916 they were twice visited by the "Guardian Angel of Portugal" or the "Angel of Peace", who spoke to them and gave them communion.

In 1925, she was visited again by the Virgin, who had a child with her, sitting on a luminous cloud. In 1926 the "Infant Jesus" came and spoke to her. In 1929 she experienced a dramatic vision, with a cross of light bearing Jesus Crucified, another figure, a chalice collecting the drops of Christ's blood, and the Virgin Mary holding her Immaculate Heart in her hand. During this vision, the Virgin Mary apparently made the important call for "the Holy Father, in union with all the Bishops of the world, to make the consecration of Russia to my Immaculate Heart, promising to save it by these means." This call for the consecration – and often conversion – of Russia has become a theme of many later visions and messages.

Only in 1941 did Lucia start writing down the contents of the "secret" she, and possibly Jacinta, had heard in the summer of 1917. She now had permission from Heaven to do so, and wrote that, "the secret is made up of three distinct parts, two of which I am now going to reveal." She said that the first part was a vision of hell – which was graphically described. This led on to the second part, that hell would be the fate of humanity if it did not mend its ways, and if Russia was not consecrated to the Immaculate Heart. Another war would start, which would "break out during the pontificate of Pius XI." The pontificate of Pius XI actually ended before the war began in 1939, but Lucia explained that the real beginning of the war was when Austria was occupied.

She also said she had been told that "When you see a night illumined by an unknown light, know that this is the great sign given you by God that He is about to punish the world for its crimes, by means of war, famine, and persecutions of the Church and of the Holy Father." This has been interpreted as a warning of the Second World War, and linked with an extraordinary occurrence of the aurora borealis on the night of January 25, 1938. Had this prophecy been written down before the event it refers to, I'd be much more impressed.

By 1942, the tension was clearly building about the content of the "Third Prophecy of Fatima", the third part of the Secret. Lucia had so far refused to tell anybody what this secret was. It appears that in June 1943 she became seriously ill, and Bishop da Silva of Fatima-Leiria, afraid the secret would never become known, asked her to write it down, and then place it inside a sealed envelope to be opened later. This she agreed to do. What happened from then on is largely a matter of conjecture, speculation, hope, faith and fear.

The most common story told about the third part of the secret is that Lucia gave the Bishop permission to read it, but he never did so. In 1957 it was taken to Rome, just as Lucia had written it, and delivered to the office of Pope Pius XII. For some reason – possibly an instruction from Lucia – he decided not to open it till 1960, but he died in 1959. By all accounts it was Pope John XXIII who opened the sealed package, probably in August 1959. He did not keep the contents entirely to himself, and there are rumours of how horrified and ashen he looked while reading it. The general expectation had been that the prophecy would refer to a nuclear conflagration leading to the end of the world. All this happened at the height of the Cold War.

But those who were waiting anxiously for the revelation of the secret and prophecy were disappointed. No hint of the content was given officially, and the end of the communiqué issued by the Vatican read something like:

"Although the Church recognises the Fatima apparitions, She does not desire to take the responsibility of guaranteeing the veracity of the words the three shepherd children said that the Virgin Mary had addressed to them."

There may be very good reasons why the Vatican – and the Pope himself – decided not to publish Lucia's account of what had been said. From my experience of messages received during visions, it seems likely that it really wasn't very sensible. It might simply have been as wrong as the prophecy that the war was ending on the day of the last vision in 1917. Or as unhelpful as prophesying in 1941 events which had taken place in 1938. Perhaps the more pragmatic officials in the Vatican realised that the messages hadn't been heard by all three children, and that what Lucia wrote in 1943 simply wasn't consistent with what the children had said during the interviews in 1917. That what the Pope had eventually read really wasn't worth bothering with.

On the other hand, it might be that Lucia's message was just so horrifying that it couldn't be released without causing panic, or risking severe damage to the Church itself. And in the way that conspiracy theories always work, it's that assumption which has achieved all the publicity. The theories put out by the believers have usually followed one of two patterns – the nuclear war/mass destruction one, or a more complicated one based on the self-destruction of the Roman Catholic Church itself. Because most of the supporters of these theories are strongly traditionalist – against married priests, in favour of the continued use of the Latin Mass – the self-destruction of the Church explanation is particularly attractive. And at the heart of it is the failure to consecrate and convert Russia, and the imminence of a great "Chastisement". We're back in an end times scenario again.

The commitment of Pope John Paul II to Fatima and its message has made a great difference to the credibility of the visions and the messages. It is said that he credits the Virgin of Fatima with his recovery after the assassination attempt, and the Church has accepted the importance of Fatima more readily since that event. But there is a great difference between the accounts of Fatima recorded before and after the additions made by Lucia's addition from 1940 onwards.

I'm still researching Fatima, and the more I look, the less I seem to find. Knowing the real contents of the Third Secret might make a difference to my attitude: for some, that problem has been resolved in a thoroughly miraculous way.

Sister Agnes of Akita, Japan

A modern visionary with a catalogue of visions to her credit, Sister Agnes reported that on October 13, 1973, the Blessed Virgin appeared to her, and revealed some of the message given to Lucia. She spoke of the Devil at work in the Church, of the "punishment greater than the Deluge" that mankind would suffer, and the unique ability of the Virgin "to save you from calamities which approach." In another vision, on September 15, 1987, the Third Secret of Fatima was again revealed, this time to Sister Agnes:

"A chastisement worse than the flood is about to come upon this poor and perverted humanity. Fire will descend from Heaven and this will be the sign that the justice of God has as of now fixed the hour of His great manifestation."

At the other end of visionary experience, in 1971 the famous American psychic Ray Stanford started to receive channelled messages from "The Source", which explained not only the content of the Fatima message, but the significance of other visions of the Virgin Mary, too, wrapped up in the usual new age vocabulary. Validating the message received from an invisible entity by one person by checking it against the message received from an invisible entity by another person leads to unimpressive standards of evidence. We'll meet similar problems again.

Garabandal

After eight introductory visits by the Archangel Michael, the Virgin Mary appeared more than 2,000 times to four girls at Garabandal, Spain between 1961 and 1965. The story of the visions, and of the investigations conducted into both the visionaries and what they saw is fascinating, but what concerns us here is the dramatic information given that this vision of the Virgin gave to the children about the future.

Here, as in most of the other Roman Catholic messages, the vision gives a clear description of a "chastisement", a horrible period of punishment and suffering to be undergone by mankind. It is similar to the Tribulation set out in the Biblical End Times scenario, but different in that it may not happen if mankind conducts itself in accordance with the instructions given by the visions.

At Garabandal, a very clear description is given of some future events that will precede the possible, or probable, "chastisement". These have become known as the "warning", the "miracle" and the "sign". The visionaries believe that after all these have occurred, the end times will be close.

The Warning is to be sent by God, and will be visible all over the world. It will be followed, at eight-thirty on a Thursday evening on the feast-day of a saint who is also a martyr of the Eucharist, by The Miracle. One of the visionaries will give eight days' notice of its arrival. It will occur over the grove of pine trees in the village, and will be seen by everyone there and in the surrounding mountains. The sick who are present will be cured, and the reigning Pope will, it seems, see it from wherever he is. Russia will be converted after The Miracle has taken place. A Sign will appear as a permanent reminder of The Miracle. It will be visible over the pines, and it will be possible to film or televise it, but not to touch it.

Because of these predictions of clear, deliberate divine interventions in the course of earthly events, Garabandal has achieved great importance in eschatology. One day in the next 3-4 years, I fully expect to hear one of the visionaries explain that The Warning has taken place, and that The Miracle is to follow. Those will be a fascinating few days for people like me.

Medjugorje

In the former territory of Yugoslavia, the visions at Medjugorje have at times become an issue in the terrible conflicts that have riven that country since it divided into the old states. The first vision took place in June 1981, witnessed by six children aged between 10 and 17. For a long time the visions appeared daily and extensive messages, including five separate "secrets", were given in the first few months alone. Most of the messages concerned prayer, penance and fasting, but there is prophecy, too. This tends to be more optimistic than other, similar visions, stressing that once there is peace in the world, as the Medjugorje vision consistently demands and prays, it will be a sure sign that God's kingdom is coming. If the sad state of Bosnia, Serbia and Croatia in recent years is anything to go by, God's kingdom is some way away yet.

The Bayside Seeress

Veronica Leuken of Bayside, New York, sometimes known as the "Bayside Seeress", started seeing visions in 1968, when St Teresa appeared to her. Over more than 20 years she has experienced visions of a wide variety of figures prominent in the Roman Catholic faith, but particularly of the Virgin Mary, and of Christ. Initially, these appeared in the grounds of an old church, but her followers later based themselves at an old World's Fair site in Flushing Meadow Park, which they named the "Vatican Pavilion".

One unusual feature of Leuken's contacts has been the publication of Polaroid photographs that appear to show mysterious lights, colours and messages. These can be interpreted in conventional ways; as misapprehensions of natural phenomena, fingers near lenses, movement of the camera and so on. However, her followers assert the genuineness of the phenomena, and fairly argue that Polaroid photos are difficult to tamper with. One photo, which clearly and boldly reads "Jacinta 1972", is said to refer to a prophecy made by one of the child visionaries from Fatima, when she was dying. It is claimed that after attending the shrine at Flushing Meadow, which Leuken's followers call "The Lourdes of America", some individuals have been cured of serious illnesses. At times, several thousand people attend the site.

The prophecies themselves are extensive, mostly appearing in the regular journal Roses. They refer to the decline of American culture and society, to the evils of rock music, the dangers of Communism, to false religions and cults, the threat presented to young people by TV programmes, to church politics, AIDS and the likely end of the world. The seeress has received messages about paranormal phenomena, too, suggesting that UFOs are not manned by extraterrestrials, or aliens as they are generally understood, but that they are the vehicles of demons and devils.

In a typical "behaviour-related" prophecy, on 6 October 1988 "Our Lady" told Veronica Leuken that "there shall not be a cure found for the disease of AIDS", but on 18 June 1990 Leuken reported that "Our Lady" had promised that if mankind repents of its satanic behaviour, then a cure for AIDS would be provided by God. In 1987 she prophesied a communist invasion of the USA from Nicaragua, through Mexico. In 1984, Jesus had appeared to her to say that, "you are fast heading for a war – the Third World War – the War that shall make mankind extinct but for the few who are chosen to keep up the Faithful and True banner before mankind." Leuken seldom gives dates, and in common with other messages received in a Roman Catholic context, the prophecies are often conditional ones – they will only come about if mankind does not dramatically change its behaviour and its attitudes to God and to prayer. Again, a message that gives me little cause for hope.

Other visions and visionaries frequently recount End Times predictions, too. In Denver, Cyndi Cain, the "Hidden Flower of the Immaculate Heart", has been receiving daily messages from the Virgin for several years. She writes vigorously of the Chastisement, and a forthcoming warning, but at the heart of her messages is the closeness of the occurrence of dramatic and frightening events.

In Betania, Venezuela, Maria Esperanza de Blanchini has been experiencing regular visions at a place now described as "The New Lourdes". Many of her messages touch on the end times, with the usual idea that they might be prevented. One typical message said, "The Great Day in which my Son will come is approaching. Pray very much so the horrible clash that is coming and that could end with so many innocents being hurt can be detained."

The Chastisement

To round off this chapter, let's focus on the heart of the end times messages received in the Roman Catholic tradition – what will the threatened, or promised, Chastisement be like? Descriptions of the Chastisement are like descriptions of Hell – which have also been quite commonplace since the experience of the children at Fatima. These descriptions come from various visionaries over the past century and a half:

"Clouds with lightning rays of fire and a tempest of fire will pass over the whole world and the punishment will be the most terrible ever known in the history of mankind. It will last 70 hours."

"An unforeseen fire will descend over the whole earth, and a great part of humanity will be destroyed."

"During a darkness lasting three days the people given to evil will perish so that only one-fourth of mankind will survive."

"He who outlives the darkness and the fear of these three days will think that he is alone on earth because the whole world will be covered by carcasses."

"Only blessed candles made of wax will give some light during this horrible darkness. One candle will last for three days, but they will not give light in the houses of the godless… all plant-life will be destroyed as well as three-fourths of the human race."

"God will send two punishments; one will be in the form of wars, revolutions and other evils; it shall originate on earth. The other will be sent from Heaven."

"The Lord God will have His day of vengeance; for his mighty sword shall be with blood. Woe unto the inhabitants of the earth; for their afflictions shall surely come, and they shall know therefore, prophets were among them and they heeded not their warnings."

I'm a little confused by the "three-day" idea, because the Chastisement in the Roman Catholic tradition seems very similar to the seven years of the Great Tribulation in the more traditional End Times Scenario, only a lot shorter. I'm wondering if this might be a good reason to consider conversion!

Chapter 7

THE FUTURE IN THE PAST

Knowledge of the future does not come only from a Christian God. There are extraordinary prophecies made hundreds of years ago that look as though they apply to our times. And there are others that appear to be ancient, but have a very uncertain pedigree. The skills and wisdom of our ancestors are particularly popular as I write, but what did they have to say about our future? And can we be sure that they really said it?

St Malachy

Take a famous name, a string of prophecies, and a 450-year gap between the death of the prophet and the first publication of his prophecies, and what do you get? Well, normally you get the sort of serious creativity that can be found with Merlin, Mother Shipton, and the Book of Daniel, but the Prophecies of St Malachy are just that little bit different.

For a start, Malachy was a real, famous person, not just a legendary one. He lived from 1094 to 1148, and was the Bishop or Archbishop of Armagh, in Ireland, and a Papal Legate. Legend has it that he died in the arms of his friend, St Bernard of Clairvaux.

Legend also has it that on his first visit to Jerusalem, Malachy had a vision of unknown origin that led to him writing down a few appropriate words about each of the 112 Popes that he considered would reign over the Church between that time and the Second Coming. Although St Bernard of Clairvaux seems to have missed this important event when writing a contemporary biography of Malachy, a book of these "prophecies" appeared in France in 1595, a listing of the 112 Popes from 1143 onwards, from Celestin II to Peter of Rome. This book did not offer the dates or lengths of their periods of office, instead giving just a few words in Latin that seemed appropriate to their personalities, to their coats of arms, or the state of the world around them. These brief lines were firmly attributed to St Malachy.

To be on the safe side, let's forget about who wrote them: there's no reason to suppose Malachy had anything to do with it. And let's forget about the 74 Popes who had already been and gone by the time the book first appeared: as prophecies, those 74 are unconvincing. Some of the descriptions given for the others seem quite meaningless – *De bona religione* for Pope Innocent XIII in 1721 means no more than, "of the good religion". Not a very telling description for a Pope. *Vir Religiosis* for Pius VIII doesn't say more than "the religious man". Many more are just as vague. But regardless of who wrote these short Latin phrases, and when, and even why, a few seem to work better than mere chance would seem to suggest would be likely. Pope Leo XIII from 1878, whose coat of arms showed a comet, was A Light In Heaven – *Lumen in Caelo*. Clement XIII, 1758, had a rose as an emblem, and was tagged with the phrase *Rosa Umbria* – Rose of Umbria or Tuscany. Pope Paul VI was *Flos Florum*, flower of flowers, and was represented by a fleur-de-lis. There are others that are as interesting.

The present Pope, John Paul II, is described by the phrase *De Labore Solis*, the labour of the sun. Apparently he was born on the day of a solar eclipse, and worked as a labourer in the open air as a young man in Poland. I don't think much of this particular piece of prediction, but it's worth noting that by the reckoning of our mysterious 16th century prophet, there are only two Popes left to go, *Gloriae Olivae* and *Petrus Romanus*. The description for Peter of Rome is the longest, reading:

"In persecutione extrema Romanae Ecclesiae sedebit Petrus romanus, qui pascet oves in multis tribulationibus, quibus transactis, civilas septicollis diruetur, et judex tremendus judicabit populum."

This means something along the lines of Peter of Rome being the Pope and feeding his people in a time of great tribulation, followed by the destruction of the city on seven hills (Rome), and the great and powerful judge coming to judge the people. A fairly neat summary of other end times scenarios.

The Malachy prophecies are intriguing. The information is so slight, yet parts of it can seem convincing. Any list of Popes compiled before the last couple of centuries would be likely to end with the Second Coming and Last Judgment, because no good Catholic writer would dare suggest that the Papacy would disappear any for any reason but the Second Coming itself. But there may be some evidence of fore-knowledge here, and I wouldn't dismiss it all too lightly.

The late, great Edgar Cayce

Edgar Cayce has long intrigued researchers into all sorts of paranormal phenomena and abilities. I've placed him among the prophets of the past not only because he seems to have been around for ever, but also because his approach, his gentlemanly attitude, makes him fit best there.

Cayce died in 1945, having consistently displayed an ability to obtain information by non-conventional means that still defies explanation by conventional science. But that ability was far more reliable in providing diagnoses for illnesses, and sometimes recommending treatments, than it was in predicting the future.

I suspect that some accounts of Cayce's achievements have become exaggerated over the years. He is mentioned, briefly, in many books and articles, but when publishers only want a few catchy sentences it's usually just the successes that appear in print – and there were failures too. It has to be pointed out that no large parts of Alabama sank underwater between 1936 and 1938. The small town of Livingston, Montana, is not an economic centre of the world. 1934 did not witness open waters appearing in northern Greenland, or new, dry lands appearing in the Caribbean. Despite the bits and pieces of rock found at Bimini, I really don't accept that the lost continent of Atlantis has been rediscovered, as Cayce predicted.

On the plus side, apart from his apparent psychism in medical matters, Cayce may have foreseen something about the Wall Street Crash, and the economic situation that led to it. He seemed to have some exceptional awareness of the rise of the Nazis, and the nations that would become involved. On a personal level, he appears to have used his presentiments to give sound business advice. It would be reasonable to suppose that if he knew some aspects of the future, he could know others.

So what did Edgar Cayce say about the future? Particularly, about the turn of this century? Well, it seems that he said quite a lot, though much of what he predicted as happening between 1958 and 1998 "when these will be proclaimed as the periods when His light will again be seen in the clouds" hasn't really turned out right. By 1998, there should have been major climatic changes, "the greater portion of Japan" should have gone into the sea. Many of the battlefields of the Second World War – during which the prophecy was made – should have "be ocean". Los Angeles and San Francisco should have been destroyed, probably followed by New York City. It seems that the southern parts of Carolina and Georgia should have disappeared under the sea already.

The predictions linked to the years 2000 and 2001 are even more dramatic. In common with others – or perhaps as the originator of an idea later heard and developed by others who knew Cayce to be unusually respected among modern prophets – he predicted a polar shift as "a logical consequence of large scale crustal displacements." The offices of those who continue to publicise Cayce's work are located in Virginia, which he believed and predicted would be safe from these upheavals. But if his predictions prove correct, there will be little comfort for any of us.

Merlin

If there's one thing we don't need, it's prophecies by someone who didn't exist, which weren't written down till several hundred years after he, er, didn't make them. Such is the case with the Merlin Prophecies, supposedly recorded by Geoffrey of Monmouth in his account of the matter of King Arthur. This is another example of what might be called "famous name" syndrome, as found in so many other prophecies where a name is plucked out of the air and some daft message attached to it. Like Daniel, John with Revelation and the other writers of traditional apocalyptic, except that Merlin's constructed prophecy is itself so decrepit as to lack even an artificial reference to modern times. To explain what I mean, a recent rendering of what Merlin is meant to have said way back in the Dark Ages comes out as:

"The hedgehog shall hoard his apples within it,
and shall make subterranean passages.
At that time shall the stones speak, and the area towards the Gaelic coast be contracted into a small space."

To be on the safe side, you'd better watch out for those apple-hoarding hedgehogs. Between them and the global warming, we're probably in real trouble.

Mother Shipton

I recently went down to the site of Mother Shipton's cave at Knaresborough, in North Yorkshire. It's a quaint and charming place. Talking to the helpful assistant in the shop there, I found that she had heard the tale that some of the good Mother's prophecies had been found in a library in Australia. I guess I shouldn't have been surprised to find that the rumour of these lost prophecies had found its way back to what, if these things ever had any reality, should have been their source.

As famous names go, Mother Shipton is nearly up there with Nostradamus and St John of Patmos. Not because of any particular prophecy she might have made, but just because she prophesied at all. She was, if you like, one of the first characters in English history to be famous just for being famous. Also, the English have always found the image of the witch intriguing and attractive and, probably quite unfairly, Mother Shipton has been given that image, too.

Like so many other "wise women" of her time – Ursula Sontheil was born in 1488 in the cave that bears her name – she appears to have had unusual abilities which the general ignorance of those around her interpreted as paranormal. She had some knowledge of healing. She seemed to have had an instinctive understanding of human psychology. She probably had some precognitive ability, which expressed itself as prophecy. In my experience, none of these things is impossible.

But even the most ardent Mother Shipton devotee has to admit that she died in 1561, and that the very first account of any of the prophecies attributed to her was published in 1641. Legends and stories were passed down locally in North Yorkshire, and there is no reason to doubt their broad truth. But like other famous people whose fame has been attached to prophecies of dubious worth, Mother Shipton has one of those great names that have always appealed to readers. And authors of prophetic pot-boilers have been around for hundreds of years.

It isn't possible to say what she did write, but we can be certain about what she didn't. She had nothing to do with "her" most famous prophecy:

"When the world to an end shall come,

In eighteen hundred and eighty-one."

This appears to have been thought up by one Charles Hindley, around the year 1850. Of course, he may have been a very unsuccessful prophet in his own right, but when 1881 came and went, the books and pamphlets were changed to say 1991. I guess that may have assured sales for another hundred years, but in the long run it was just another failure.

Because of the hundred or more years between the making of the prophecies that might have really been made, and when they were written down, this is another situation where the events had taken place before the earliest records we have. They seem to have been recorded in prose, not in the catchy little rhymes produced in the past 200 years:

"Iron in the water shall float

As easy as a wooden boat;

Carriages without horses shall go.

And accidents fill the world with woe.

Under water men shall walk,

Shall ride, shall sleep, shall talk.

In the air men shall be seen,

In white, in black, and in green."

We never will know quite why Mother Shipton achieved her reputation as a prophet, but we do have these mysterious prophecies from the secret depths of an Australian library. They have now been published twice in *Nexus* magazine, which explained that:

"This rare collection of Mother Shipton's prophecies was sent to us by a *Nexus* reader who told us that, 30 years ago, she painstakingly transcribed them and managed to smuggle them out of the Mitchell Library, Sydney (now the State Library of New South Wales). The originals were kept in a locked room, along with many other volumes of prophetic writings deemed unsuitable for viewing by the general public."

Perhaps the simple facts about Mother Shipton never reached Australia. Along with verses published in the past 200 years in Britain – supposedly held in the library written on *scrolls*, there are four, four-line rhymes, supposedly "found on a scroll in a separate jar", which could be said to predict the prevalence of AIDS. Silliest of all there were the trite verses found "on the outer wrapping of the scrolls", supposedly signed by Mother Shipton herself. I rather suspect that whoever provided these gems to *Nexus* magazine had seen the witch-like picture of Mother Shipton and jumped to the conclusion that she had, consequently, been burned to death:

"I know I go, I know I'm free

I know that this will come to be.

Secreted this, for this will be

Found by later dynasty.

A dairy maid, a bonny lass

Shall kick this tome as she does pass

And five generations she shall breed

Before one male child does learn to read.

This is then held year by year

Till an iron monster trembling fear
Eats parchment, words and quill and ink
And mankind is given time to think.
And only when this comes to be
Will mankind read this prophecy
But one man's sweet's another's bane
So I shall not have burned in vain."

I'm beginning to see what the Bible meant about being wary of false prophets.

Pyramid Prophecies

As the explorers among us find there is little new left in the present, more and more mysteries are being found in the past. This isn't difficult, because what's left of most ancient civilisations is stones and artefacts, with few words of any real significance. You can make pretty much what you want of the meaning of stones, and if you're good at it your discoveries can appear quite brilliant.

One of the neatest routes to fame and fortune is to think of an ancient artefact – real or imagined, it doesn't much matter – and then write a book about looking for it. The really subtle writers don't actually find the thing – the classic is ending up, helpless, just the wrong side of a church door from a prized religious symbol that probably never took the shape and form in which the author was apparently searching for it in the first place. If you see what I mean. Less subtle have been recent quests for items like the Holy Grail, or the whole "Ancient Astronaut" scenario, where a carving of a man with a ring round his head becomes an alien in a space helmet, and everything is something far more special than anyone but the author had ever considered. Not subtle at all is "psychic questing", hopefully a uniquely British activity in which small groups of excited people find objects that nobody knew were missing, and which somehow don't get submitted for scientific analysis. I can't say this doesn't make a lot of people very happy, but that's people for you.

I'm not an "ancient wisdom" person. I'm mostly interested in people really fulfilling their potential. What people can know, and what people can do. While I have great respect for, say, the builders of Stonehenge, the Pyramids or Carnac, or even Westminster Abbey or the Cathedral at Chartres, my respect is based on their technical skill in an age of ignorance, not on any admiration for their personal beliefs and religious convictions. People have been building monstrously complex, time-consuming and expensive monuments to their gods for many thousands of years, and their gods continue to show the same disinterest they always have, letting us get on with destroying each other. Actually, people have usually been made to built the monuments by other people. When I think of the Pyramids, I associate them with year after year of merciless slave labour. The great ancient cities of South America with cruel and pointless human sacrifice. Nice buildings, shame about the brutality.

But thanks to a lot of sacrifice and a little inspiration, there are plenty of monuments around, and where there's monuments there's interpretation, and where there's interpretation, there's prophecy. We're really in the thick of this as we approach 2000.

The Great Pyramid

Amazing alignments and astronomical accuracy aside, and with due respect to those who have feted those issues, for a big pile of stones the Great Pyramid seems to have a lot to say, and it's been saying it for a long time now.

Actually, the Great Pyramid was probably the first man-made artefact, apart from the Temple at Jerusalem, to become an object used for the factual interpretation of information. It is a building marvellously full of fascinating shapes and passages, of different finishes of stone and materials, passages that rise and fall, and widen and narrow, and lead into and out of chambers. Some of those chambers, virtually inaccessible and likely to be explored by small motorised drones carrying cameras, may yet hold mysteries as remarkable as the treasure of Tutankhamun. But has the Pyramid already yielded far greater wonders than that?

There are many different systems of interpretation, but most are linear, tracing along one passage or another, looking at heights, lengths, how rough or smooth or finished they are, and then matching dates and events to the lengths, heights, differences and changes. Sometimes inscriptions and drawings are used to expand on the "timeline" prophecies. It's not something that I, personally, would ever have thought of by myself, but it's been fascinating some intelligent and interesting minds for well over a century. I don't have the space here to explain how these systems work. To be honest, some of them are quite baffling. But we need to know what prophecies have been made, and what they promise for our future.

Let's start at that point, before we backtrack. Dr Joseph Robert Jochmans (he has an "honorary" Doctorate of Literature from Northgate Graduate School in Washington, a "center for specialised Biblical research") writes about and publicises prophecies of all kinds, but for the Great Pyramid he chooses to base his interpretations on the recently republished work of Peter Lemesurier, author of *The Great Pyramid Decoded*.

Lemesurier was not the first to use a measure termed the "pyramid inch" to represent one year of human history, and using this measurement he traces a "time line" through the internal features of the pyramid, towards the King's Chamber. He actually finds indications in this system of events to come as late as the 83rd century, but Jochmans concludes the next significant historical event indicated in the Pyramid's structure is marked by "where the limestone floor in the Antechamber ends, and the Aswan granite floor begins". He feels that the change from a "dead to an energy-living stone… can only signify a major quantum leap in the spiritual development of future humanity" to begin to occur on "February 21, 1999".

This is how Pyramid prophecy works, and the stage after identifying when an event will happen is to identify what that event will be. In this particular instance, Jochmans speculates that the event will be the discovery, under the Great Pyramid and the Sphinx, of a "Lost Hall of Records", an event he thinks was predicted by Herodotus, and various other ancient historians. He also thinks it was predicted by Nostradamus, though the quatrain he adopts to support this proposition is interpreted by Cheetham as referring to the transactions of the French National Assembly, 22 December 1789, and by Roberts as, "A corrupt period in history, when too many sects will spring up, creating great conflict in the Church." For Jochmans, the significance of this discovery is that the knowledge and information contained therein will dramatically change mankind's spirituality, and "will cause all world philosophies to be turned upside down."

This particular step in the time line is just one typical example of how a small feature in a remarkable building is interpreted as a sign of the end of the world as we know it. You will find that this is just one of many.

What Jochmans will not tell you about – and nor will any other of the modern pyramid prophets – is that this has all been done before. As I mentioned, the Great Pyramid was an early subject of the interpreters of physical mysteries, at a time when the new age/ancient wisdom/lost knowledge movement wasn't more than a glint in the eye of Madame Blavatsky. But then, in a wonderful combination of absolutely different philosophies, the greatest monument of a pagan, heliocentric, god-man religion was used to predict an absolutely standard, fundamentalist Christian End Times scenario.

Nothing conveys pyramid prophecy as well as a quote, here from 1924 and *The Great Pyramid – Its Spiritual Symbolism*, one of several beautifully produced books on the subject from this period:

"The King's Chamber indicates the date of the Second Advent of Jesus Christ, 1874 AD. (The actual Pyramid-inch measurement, as indicated in the diagram, is 3687.105+. This corresponds to the period of 3687 years from Jacob's death in 1813 BC to 1874 AD, taking these two dates as whole numbers).

"Since Christ's return in 1874 he has been engaged as Chief Reaper in the harvest work of gathering the wheat (the saints) into the garner, and binding the tares (professing Christians) in bundles ready to be burned as tares, ie to be manifested as not true Christians. Soon Satan will be completely bound, and the kingdoms of this world completely overthrown in the great time of trouble which began as foretold in 1914 AD; and Christ's reign will eventually bring in everlasting peace."

The 1914 date was found by starting a measurement of 1915 pyramid inches from the "Pyramid's Socket-level base line" and taking a rather complicated route to the "upper terminal of the Grand Gallery". This measurement business isn't always simple, but for these interpreters 1914 was the end of the period of the times of the Gentiles, when Jesus Christ "exercised his Divinely conferred right and assumed Kingly authority as Earth's new (invisible) Ruler."

I'm not convinced that this generation of prophets had predicted that Earth's new ruler would be "(invisible)". I think they'd expected something more obvious and convincing, and they'd certainly expected the Millennium to begin in 1914, and to end in 2914 AD. By the time of the appearance of *The Great Pyramid – Its Divine Message* in 1948, the invisibility was becoming a bit of a worry, but it only required a little recalculation to work out that 1914 was "the commencement of chaos" and that it was "the ushering in of the Epoch of chaos preceding the Messianic 1000 years." To put it another way, the Millennium was postponed by the introduction of two periods of chaos with a period of truce in the middle, because the Low Passage between the Grand Gallery and the King's Chamber was divided into two portions. These changes covered the period from 1914 to 1936, and then from 1936 to 1953 there was a "period of the Judgment of the Nations", which was going on when the book was written. However, it's clear the Millennium didn't begin in 1953, regardless of what the Great Pyramid had to say.

All of which may suggest to you why the current generation of Pyramid prophets doesn't tell you about the last generation. But that isn't going to stop the speculation, or the measuring and the calculation. Both the Pyramids and the Sphinx are mighty and wonderful objects, and we'll hear a lot more about them in the next few years. Of course, it's just possible that US prophet Gordon-Michael Scallion may be right in the complex visions he had concerning the links between the Egyptian monuments and the future. He describes the approach to the Great Hall, its contents, how it was built, how it's protected by machines and sensors, and records all sorts of astonishing events and achievements. He also says that in a vault, in the atrium of the Great Hall, details of the identities of present and future incarnations of Hermes, Ra, Isis, and various other Egyptian luminaries will be found written down. Let's all hope their reincarnated forms are a lot less ruthless, a lot less keen on slavery and enforced labour, than they were first time around.

The Knowledge of the Mayans

Recent material that appeared under the catchy heading of "Mayan prophecies" has proved to be pretty much the usual "ancient knowledge" mixture, stringing together Atlantis, Egypt, Christ, Edgar Cayce and Crystal Skulls. Several of the New Age favourites, but overlaid with an investigation into the Mayan calendar, its period and significance.

The Mayans supposedly divided their history into vast cycles – good, Theosophical stuff, with civilisations rising and falling explained by events including pole shifts and comets. Supposedly, the last Great Cycle ended, and the current one began, on August 13, 3114 BC by the Gregorian calendar. The significance of that date beyond being a symbolic "birth of Venus" seems to have baffled even the Mayan experts, and I understand that it was only arrived at, by calculation rather than any original memory or record, within the past 1,000 years. There seems to be quite a gap there.

Anyway, the same cycle that started in 3114 BC finishes, it seems, in 2012 AD, although that doesn't seem to be a prophecy of total destruction. Yes, the date given is close to 2000, but it does seem to be a very old prediction, based on a system that specified the way in which natural events should be understood, rather than one that involved any genuine prophetic ability or foreknowledge on the part of any person who might understand our futures. This prophecy actually seems to be based on a particular conjunction of planets visible from Mayan sites in 2012, but I think that all the evidence we have to date suggests that conjunctions don't actually move as much as a piece of chewing-gum from its normal pattern of behaviour, let alone an entire world.

I suggest that what was amazing to the Mayans should, if we kept our sense of proportion, and the awareness of our hugely superior scientific knowledge, be quite unamazing to us. Stars conjoin. Comets appear. Eclipses make parts of the world go dark for a while. While it may be impressive, if true, that the Mayans could forecast a conjunction a thousand years ahead, it seems foolish to take on their interpretation of the significance of that event. It appears to be an impressive piece of calculation, but as prophecies go it's more an anachronism than a threat.

As for the current popularity of the "Mayan" "crystal skulls", it seems that in legend they were brought to Earth by the Sky People during the Third World of Water, over 75,000 years ago when all the world's land was one continent. It is said that 13 crystal skulls will come together in the land of their origin, where they will reveal the mysteries of the universe and save mankind. Just how isn't yet clear. In view of recent research on the Skulls, which will be blithely ignored by those who believe in their power, it seems that both skulls and legends may well be of quite recent manufacture.

Hopi Prophecies

I decided to report to you on the prophecies of the Hopi tribe of native North Americans, because I keep on finding references to the "Hopi Prophecies". On closer inspection, these mostly seem to derive from the Internet, which I'm fast realising is an absolute curse when it comes to trying to check the truth of anything that appears on it. It seems as though what does appear is the opinion of one or two individuals, who may or may not be representative of the Hopi Nation. At a guess, I'd say they probably aren't representative: most of the esoteric material on the net seems to be there because you can reach more people that way than by holding meetings in rented halls saying you're in touch with people from space, or walking around with sandwich boards declaring "The End of the World is Nigh".

Anyway, working from this rather unsound basis, it seems that Hopi prophecy works around a principle of cyclical change common to many cultures, and that they, too, are involved in looking for various "signs of the times" which will signify a "great purification" or something similar. Not a total end, but an imminent, dramatic earth change which the Hopi will survive.

One version, which bears all the hallmarks of being a friend of a friend tale at best, is attributed to "White Feather, a Hopi of the ancient Bear Clan", in a conversation with "a minister named David Young" driving through New Mexico in 1958, but published in 1980 by the same Joseph Robert Jochmans who brought us the Great Hall of Records as prophesied by Nostradamus. White Feather gives Young some ancient prophecies, a sequence of Nine Signs signifying that "the Fourth World shall end soon, and the Fifth World will begin." The First Sign was the coming of the white men, the Fourth that the "prairie will be crossed by snakes of iron" (you guessed, railways), the Fifth, "the land shall be criss-crossed by a giant spider's web", interpreted by Young in 1958 as meaning "the telephone and electric lines that flashed past alongside the highway". Seven referred to the poisoning of the sea, and Eight was "You will see many youth, who will wear their hair long like my people, come and join the tribal nations to learn of their ways and wisdom." Both would have been clever in 1958, old hat in 1980.

The Ninth and last sign was that, "You will hear of a dwelling-house in the heavens, above the Earth, that shall fall with a great crash. It will appear as a Blue Star. Very soon after this, the ceremonies of my people will cease. These are the Signs that great destruction is coming. The world shall rock to and fro..." Essentially, White Feather predicts nuclear war, before those who survive see "the Emergence, into the Fifth World."

Oddly enough Australian prophet Stan Deyo, a keen advocate and user of the Internet, reports having a chance encounter with a girl in a CD shop in Arizona early in 1996, which led him to a high-powered and mystical meeting with Chief Augustine Mawa of the Shungopavi. It seems that they told him about the coming earth changes, and "a prophecy they have which told of the time when a webbing would be all over the land and it would signal the approach of the 'great purification' leading into the age of the fifth world of mankind on earth." You won't be amazed to hear that Deyo had seen this webbing in a dream, and was able to interpret this sign for the Hopi. "I had come to show them things from that web on a small computer and in doing so, I had assisted them in interpreting one of their signs for these times..." I guess he hadn't read the Australian magazine in which the piece by Jochmans about White Feather and the minister was published in 1995. Surprising, perhaps, when Deyo himself lives in Australia, and appears and advertises regularly in that magazine.

Mitar Tabarich

Straight from a page on the World Wide Web, and just possibly from 19th-century Serbia comes, a report of a prophet who, if the tale told is true, was remarkably able. That "if" might, in the nature of the Internet, be a particularly important one, and it could be that by the time you come to read this summary of his prophecies for the future, the whole thing will be a proven hoax. More likely, as with other myths that people want to believe in, it will keep on turning up in different places, till eventually it looks as though it's real. I haven't, personally, come across this prophecy in this form before.

The story goes that the prophet in this case was Mitar Tarabich, an illiterate peasant from a Serbian village called Kremna. He apparently lived from 1829 to 1899, and when he experienced his prophetic visions (nothing is said about what form they took) he would recount them to his godfather, a Serbian Orthodox priest who wrote down Mitar's prophecies in a small notebook "which was damaged by fire in 1943 when his family house was destroyed by the occupying Bulgarian Army." The priest was born in 1836, so there is a small mystery in a person being the godson of someone seven years his junior. However, Serbian Orthodoxy may have its own particular customs; the remains of the notebook now seem to be "in the possession of the family of the priest's grandson". Addresses don't come into it, nor the route by which the prophecies found their way onto the Internet.

As you might have guessed, Mitar's prophecies of events that had occurred when the prophecies were first published are often brilliantly accurate, particularly about what happened in and around Serbia from 1903 onwards. But that isn't really much of a test. For the future as of now, from 1996 onwards, he has specific prophecies that parallel many others. There will, it seems, be evil men who:

"will poison air and water and spread pestilence over the seas, rivers and earth, and people will start to die suddenly of various ailments... men will start to die in great numbers. Then people will run away from cities to the country and look for the mountains with three crosses and there, inside, they will be able to breathe and drink water, but not for long because a great famine will appear. There will be plenty of food in towns and villages, but it will be poisoned. Many will eat because of hunger and die immediately."

"We (Serbia) will not fight in this war, but others will do battle over our heads. Burning people will fall from the sky over Pozega... Only one country at the end of the world, surrounded by great seas, as big as our Europe, will live in peace, without any troubles. Upon it or over it, not a single cannonball will explode!"

You might think that this last reference could only mean Australia. Oddly enough, the account of "The Prophetic Visions of Mitar Tabarich" appears in *Nexus*, an Australian magazine.

Chapter 8

THERE'S NOTHING WORSE THAN
A GOD WHO GETS HIS FACTS WRONG

Every prophecy that placed the end of the world before the end of July, 1996 has, as I write, been demonstrably wrong. There are those who say that the Antichrist is alive here or there, preparing for his time to come. Others claim that the Messiah, or Maitreya, appears from time to time in much the way that do visions and aliens, obscurely and untestably, reported on some time after the event. But we can't escape the simple fact that there is a vast amount of prophecy that has clearly been proved wrong. Some because it was deliberately false, much because those who distributed it were dismally mistaken.

Many millennial groups and movements start with the belief that if information seems to come from beyond or outside Earth, then it must be right. Unfortunately, that isn't necessarily so, and there are many examples from this century of just how wrong that belief can be. Here are a few case histories that range from the sad to the downright dangerous, representing all kinds of entities and sources of knowledge, all of which turned out not to have a clue about the future.

The No-War Prophecies

Prophecy and prediction by illustrious entities from other realms has become commonplace in recent years, but in Britain in 1938 it was a rare event. Though Spiritualism was at the height of its popularity, most of the messages given through mediums were about the facts of life after death, or attempted to prove the survival of specific individuals. Communications from the dead, and from "guides" – often Native Americans or wise old Chinese – were taken seriously. Their messages appeared in the weekly papers *Psychic News* and *Two Worlds*.

Against a background of growing Nazi aggression, what became known as the "No-War Prophecies" began. In March 1938 White Hawk, the guide of medium Kathleen Barkel, declared, "For some years now I have told you there will be no war in your country... The day of reckoning for the dictators is not far away." Silver Birch, who spoke through *Psychic News* editor Maurice Barbanell, said that, "A new era is gradually dawning for humanity", and many other communicators agreed.

Two months before Hitler invaded Czechoslovakia, the spirit world remained convinced there would be no war. Red Cloud asserted that,

"We have returned from the spirit world to succeed and not to fail", and Britain's leading Spiritualist added, "the radiant light will shine upon a world bathed in the glories of peace before the year 1939 has passed."

Late in July, as Europe slid towards war, *Psychic News* stayed firm. "I am confident there is no possibility of error when the prophecy is so unanimous. From every well known guide and from home circles all over the world there has come the assurance that never again will England be involved in war."

Twelve days before war began the late Earl Haig, the British commander in the First World War, returned from the Other Side to say, "The present crisis will be over within 14 days. The physical danger is over now." Through a spirit guide called Bert, former newspaper magnate Lord Northcliffe agreed. Sadly, because of printing and publication dates, the final "no war" predictions actually appeared in print after the war had begun. There was, of course, nothing wrong in hoping that the inevitable wouldn't occur, but it took years for Spiritualism to recover from its misplaced confidence in discarnate entities.

Disappointment from Planet Clarion

The boundaries between believing in gods, spirits and alien beings are hard to define, and there is often little real difference. Like the Millerites more than 100 years earlier, the story of "Marian Keech" and the beings from the planet Clarion gives us the chance to look at an end times cult in detail. The full story can be found in the classic book *When Prophecy Fails*, which was written by three sociologists – Leon Festinger, Henry Riecken and Stanley Schachter. They "planted" observers in a group led by a woman who produced automatic writing to receive increasingly complex messages. For their research, they called her "Marian Keech", and her home town "Lake City".

Keech first made contact with her late father, but in a pattern of contact with non-human intelligences that I've seen occur elsewhere, this was followed first by messages from "the Elder Brother", and then from entities who lived on the planets Clarion and Cerus, neither of which are known to astronomers. In particular, she received messages from an entity from Clarion called Sananda, who claimed to have previously been Jesus Christ. As we'll see, the Sananda-Jesus link is currently common in channelling circles, and the communicator now calling himself Sananda is often identified by a stylised "picture" of the traditional, westernised Christ. I wonder if that tradition began here?

In August 1954, although Keech wasn't keen on publicity, the growing group's first press release was issued. The philosophy of the group was of little interest to the press, but the prediction of an imminent major physical disaster was. By September, the information on that aspect had become more specific, and the *Lake City Herald* reported that:

"Lake City will be destroyed by a flood from Great Lake just before dawn, December 21st, according to a suburban housewife. Mrs Marian Keech says the prophecy is not her own. It is the purport of many messages she has received by automatic writing... sent to her by superior beings from a planet called Clarion. These beings have been visiting the Earth, she says, in what we call "Flying Saucers". During their visits, she says, they have observed fault lines in the Earth's crust that foretoken the deluge. Mrs Keech reports she was told the flood will spread to form an inland sea stretching from the Arctic Circle to the Gulf of Mexico."

By this time, Keech was communicating with "The Guardians", as well as Sananda. She told her followers that if they did the right things and were gathered together, ready, at the appointed time, they would not be drowned in the coming flood, but would be rescued by one or more flying saucers. The group was also faced with a problem caused by the number of visitors it was receiving. The extraterrestrials could come at any time, and in any way, and the group not only had to decide whether or not visitors were ETs, but also whether they were good or evil ETs!

As December 21st drew closer, members of the group gave up jobs, possessions and relationships, and some took up unusual diets. One condition made by the Guardians was that those to be rescued should have no metal on them, which led to some interesting arrangements with regard to brassieres, and holding up trousers. Dental fillings caused a lively discussion!

Over the final days, increasingly strange messages and predictions were received, all of which proved to be inaccurate. The group became confused, but remained faithful and determined. Come the day itself there was no flood, and no spacecraft. After a while the group dispersed, disappointed and disillusioned. If somebody now, 40 years on, conducted similar research, I suspect they'd observe very similar patterns of behaviour in any group that depends on a particular day, and a promised event, for its reason to exist.

Jeane Dixon

One of the great self-publicists, Jeane Dixon has made so many prophecies that I guess that some of them have to turn out right. In *My Life and Prophecies*, published in 1969, she takes the reader into both past and future, from the private life of Queen Nefertiti to the birth of the Antichrist in 1962. She sets out a very Christian, but dateless, end times scenario.

She also predicted that the USA would have a woman president in the 1980s, that Bernadette Devlin has a "brilliant future", that "we can begin to withdraw our soldiers and let the South Vietnamese fight and win their war against the Communists", that "President Nixon is our last hope". Years ago, she saw the imminent death of Fidel Castro, leader of Cuba.

The most specific "end of the world as we know it" prediction Dixon made was firmly in the tradition of prophets both ancient and modern. I suppose that in 1969 the 1980s were far enough away not to worry too much about, and she wrote that: "I have seen a comet strike our Earth around the middle of the 1980s. Earthquakes and tidal waves will befall us as a result of this heavenly body in one of our great oceans. It may well become known as one of the worst disasters of the 20th century. I will provide a more detailed warning at a future date." More recently, writing of OJ Simpson, she predicted: "I don't see him walking away until an appeal." I shan't be worrying about any futures predicted by Ms Dixon.

Something to do, somewhere to go

Two UFO-based groups from the USA showed early signs of New Age thinking, as well as predicting dramatic earth changes.

The Light Affiliates were active in the late 1960s in Burnaby, British Columbia. Their launching statement read:

"We wish to notify all those interested that a phenomenon has occurred here in Vancouver. A young girl, age 22, suddenly began channelling on 23.10.69. Her source is a being identifying himself as 'Ox-Ho', who is relaying transmissions from a galaxy close to our own... Her material is phenomenal in that she has been informed of the coming disasters, when to expect them, and what to do pertaining to the necessary evacuation of the danger areas and food supplies, etc. that will be needed."

The real name of the "channel" was Robin McPherson, but in a style commonly adopted by more recent channellers, she was renamed "Estelle" by the "being". Her mother Ailen became "Magdalene", her friend Sally became "Celeste". A young man involved in the early communications was given the evocative name of "Truman Merit".

Ox-Ho (yes, I know it's hard to take this one seriously) had explained that the day of judgment would begin on 22 November 1969. In these final remaining hours, mankind would be "given a last opportunity to repair his decadent house before the terminal series of disasters". If mankind missed this chance to change, "the Space Brothers would remove the Chosen and return them to Earth after the planet had once again "crystallised", and been spiritually, as well as physically, restructured". The "restructuring" would involve the tilting of Earth on its axis, and the disappearance beneath the sea of large areas of land.

As you'll know, the day of judgment didn't begin in November 1969. Robin McPherson was interviewed about her mission a few years later, when she explained that she had misinterpreted the visions of destruction that she had seen.

She said: "The thing is that it is the first ascension. The Brothers are trying to get as many people as possible into the Kingdom... You know, I've been told by the Brotherhood that Earth is like an encounter therapy centre for the psychotics of the Universe."

"An encounter therapy centre for the psychotics of the Universe." Now, that's what I call *real* wisdom. I think I could find substantial evidence to support that contention!

Bo and Peep – previously known as MH Applewhite and Bonnie Nettles – went a step further than just communicating with discarnate entities. They formed a group called Human Individual Metamorphosis (HIM) in California in 1975, and achieved a sizeable following. This middle-aged man and woman advertised their public meetings with posters that said, "Two individuals say they were sent from the level above human and will return to that level in a spaceship (UFO) within the next three months."

The basis of the cult was that if its followers conducted themselves within the strict rules set out by Bo and Peep, giving up names and possessions, drugs, alcohol, radio, television, sex, books and personal relationships, then the followers could ascend with them to the level above human. Their teachings offered the advantages of life after death without the inconvenience of dying. Sadly, this was an attractive prospect to some of the lost souls emerging from the drug culture, seeking personal spiritual development and some element of certainty in their lives. It sounds like what we used to call a "power trip" for Applewhite and Nettles.

Early in their mission, the ascended visitors had claimed that one day they would be assassinated, and then be resurrected after three days. However, before they or anyone else rose to any other realm, it became known that they had actually met each other in a psychiatric hospital where he was a patient, and she a nurse. The movement eventually ground to a halt despite the continuing support of some of those who believed in it. Although the pair of them reappeared a year or two ago, so far as I'm aware their return met with little response.

The members of the Lighthouse Gospel Tract Foundation of Tucson, Arizona were firm believers in the physical reality of the Biblical Rapture, and had no doubt it would take place on 28 June 1981. Like others who used the "date verses" in the book of Daniel to calculate that Christ would return 40 years after the foundation of Israel in 1948, and that there would have to be seven years for the Tribulation between the Rapture and the Second Coming, the Foundation fixed on the date in 1981. The Foundation's President, Bill Maupin, said: "We will slowly rise from the ground and in our bodies drift into the cloud. Every human who has been saved will rise in the lift-off. Cemeteries all over the world will come alive. The saved will stand up from their graves in the bodies they had before they died. Those saved will go on a one-way trip for six or seven years, and then we will be coming back. People will ascend into heaven towards the evening of 28 June."

The commitment of his followers was noted by the media. A doctor gave up his job, and disposed of his Porsche. His wife sold her boutique. Others had sold their homes, or decided not to renew leases on rented property. When the day passed without event, group members blamed themselves, not God, for the error. They remained confident that the Rapture would still happen.

The Holy Ground Mission in Frankston, Texas, predicted a similar date for the Second Coming, choosing 18 September 1988. In 1979 the group were already living a simple, communal life, about 40 adults and 30 children, managing without modern power sources because, "we have been called to restore all things to the original paths". Intriguingly Tom Crotser, the group's leader, was previously a professional stage magician, who had committed himself to rediscovering Biblical arte-facts in the belief that this task had to be completed before the Second Coming. He had travelled to Turkey nine times, and claimed not only to have found the remains of Noah's Ark on Mount Ararat, but also to have discovered the remnants of the Tower of Babel there, and not in Iraq where it was usually believed to have been located.

Less comfortable were the Sunshiners, a 25-strong church group in Grannis, Arkansas who in December 1975 had been staying in a small, three-bedroomed house for more than two months, refusing to come out. A spokesman for the group explained: "We met here for a prayer meeting on the night of 29 September, and the Lord directed us to stay here, inside this house, and told us He would be coming any time. He told us to tarry and wait. So we've been here ever since, and we expect to stay. We pray together and hold hands. There's no ritual, and no churches involved, and nothing crazy about it."

South Korea, 28 October 1992

I never know quite what to believe about the preparations believers supposedly make when they're expecting to be taken away from the earth by one mysterious means or another. Is it really the journalists who, you might say, are getting carried away, or is there no limit to the sacrifices that can be made?

The Marian Keech story from the fifties seemed far-out enough to me, with the debate among her followers about whether the instruction to have no metal on them when they boarded the flying saucer meant they should remove the metal fillings from their teeth. But then I found an article in *The Washington Times* for 29 October 1992 about the Dami Mission Church in South Korea. Apart from the usual distribution and sale of possessions, not only did it claim that these good Christians, expecting to be physically raptured, took "martial-arts classes so they could kick away people who might try to hold on to them as they flew upward", but also, "women reportedly had abortions to make them-selves lighter". If true, that's among the saddest things I've ever heard. If not, the journalist should be ashamed of himself for writing it.

Yet the South Korean rapture prophecy – which failed to unfold on 28 October 1992 – was one of the best-supported this century. Based on the religious experiences of three Korean teenagers, about 250 churches, with 20,000 members became involved in a passionate certainty that the world would end that midnight, and then had to face reporters outside their churches as they went home, still faithful, but disappointed. It may be worth noting that the founder of the Church at the heart of the prophecy wasn't able to be with his followers that night. He was in custody, awaiting trial on charges of misappropriating church funds, and the illegal possession of foreign currency, and the Minister of the Mission for the Coming Days had to stand in for him.

Harold Camping

Being mistaken about the date of Christ's return isn't limited to those who are otherwise unsuccessful or easily persuaded. In 1992 Harold Camping announced that the return would occur between September 15 and September 27, 1994. Camping owned the Family Radio network of Christian radio stations in the USA, and had his own nightly show. He detailed his predictions in two books, *1994?* and *Are You Ready?*

Using those "date verses" in Daniel again, he worked out that the creation of the world had taken place exactly 13,000 years before May 1988, and that Satan had been loosed from his captivity on the 22nd of that month. The 2,300 days mentioned in Daniel 8:14 were the period of Tribulation – unusually not much over six years – between then and the return. Which took humanity to September 1994. I'm not sure what happened to the Rapture in this scheme!

Although he was challenged by other evangelists, Camping took a very firm line. He inaugurated his own church, announced that all believers should leave churches which practised speaking in tongues, and that those who did not would be "killed" by Satan. He also stated that nobody could be saved after 6 September 1994. I understand that 80,000 copies of the books were produced, and that the income of Family Radio from gifts rose by 15-20 per cent as the appointed day approached. When it came and went, he apparently suspected miscalculation, and that his prophecy would still be fulfilled before the end of 1994. At least he didn't appear to have done any great harm.

Chapter 9

ARMED AND DANGEROUS

The Waco Tragedy

You might expect me to write a lot about Waco, but I don't think I really know what happened there. Bizarre and entertaining as much of the world of millennial belief may be, with at least 85 people who lived with the Branch Davidians dead in the tragic fire at the end of what was pretty much a siege, and a further six Branch Davidians and four government agents dead in the gunfight that led to that siege, this isn't one to joke about. It was probably as close as you get to a massacre in the democratic, Western world, and it still doesn't make much sense.

Rather like the stories and rumours about the Oklahoma bombing, which will continue regardless of any verdict brought in by a court, I doubt that we'll ever understand what went on in and among the Branch Davidians. Their leader was David Koresh, known till near the end of his life as Vernon Howell. "Koresh" appears to have been adapted from "Cyrus", the Persian King who showed favour to the exiled Jews, but Howell explained that it was also a name for God, and meant "death", too.

Most of the media interest in the Branch Davidians – a distant relation to the Seventh Day Adventists, and vague descendants of William Miller and the Millerites of the 1840s – arose from allegations to do with sex. Not much new there. But it does seem that Koresh did to excess what other cult leaders did only from time to time. Even before the siege at Waco began, an Australian private detective had conducted a thorough investigation lasting eight months, and came up with allegations of sex with a child of 12, and being the father of many of the children living within the cult. Koresh talked openly and deliberately about his sexual activities, and he appears to have been cruel, exploitative and obsessed with his own perfection. Yet he was loved and nearly worshipped. What sense does that make?

I'd guess that Koresh believed in his own propaganda, and that as he developed from being a mere spokesman for Christ to being something very like Christ himself, he retained that conviction. I don't think that men like Koresh often calculate their debauchery from the outset, planning what they'll do on the basis of what they might get out of it. Anyway, I doubt that would work.

Real conviction has real attractions, and while I can't say that the film of him I've seen does a great deal for me, most of Koresh's converts came from similar religious groups to the Branch Davidians, people who already had expectations of the End Times, and who knew their Bibles. Bible exposition seems to have been Koresh's other great talent, and he could talk, harangue even, for hours. In a world where that skill counted for a lot, Koresh was able to win followers with little difficulty.

Beyond that, as time went on he became increasingly confident about his role in the End Times. Very much a Book of Revelation man, he set himself in a position where he could persuade his followers that he had total control over the unfolding of the end of the world. The role he took was that of the "Lamb" in Revelation, who appears to have control over the opening of the Seven Seals, setting the end in motion with their attendant horrors. Neatly, the "Lamb" was also an image that was given to Christ himself, and while the claim to being Christ himself may not have been originally attended by Koresh, when he was asked the crucial "Are you Christ?" question, he was just too involved to say no.

As I've said, we don't really know much about the relationship between Koresh and his followers. We don't know what his followers really expected would happen when they went into seclusion at Waco, how they regarded the first round of shooting, what they were thinking as they died by fire. There has been little investigation of cult members who haven't lost their faith, which is a pity. Disillusioned cult members tell remarkably similar stories, but we could do with understanding the relationship followers have with a leader who really believes he is the Lamb from the Book of Revelation, or has the power to open the Seven Seals, and bring about the Last Judgment. I guess that everyday custom, and logic and reason become redundant, and a passion and excitement take over that few of us can understand. Koresh was, of course, wrong about who he was, about what he could do, where he should be and who should be with him. But I rather hope the passion and excitement was still in place at Waco, as something very close to a massacre took place.

The White Brotherhood

Just how easily vulnerable people become attracted to irrational beliefs is demonstrated in the rise and fall of the White Brotherhood in Kiev, in the Ukraine, in 1993. In the aftermath of the break-up of the Soviet

Union, the social and economic certainties of centralised Communism disappeared. Food prices shot up, and life became unstable and unpredictable. Religious freedom brought a new kind of choice.

Under Communism belief and worship had always been possible, if difficult, but opposition can give strength and coherence to a faith, and to those who follow it. The states of the former Soviet Union have seen all sorts of cults and religions come and go in recent years, but none have achieved the notoriety of the White Brotherhood – perhaps because it attracted young people in a country where religious belief was traditionally the preserve of the old.

It was a classic doomsday cult, with a lot of Christian trappings. Masterminded by a manipulative older man called Yuri Krivonogov – who would only answer to the name Johann Swami – and fronted by the young and attractive Marina Tsvyguna, usually known as Maria Devi Khristos, it adapted several elements from Biblical apocalyptic.

Maria had made it clear that she was either the reincarnation of Jesus, or the earthly incarnation of God, and the cult's key prediction was that on 11 November 1993, Maria would be crucified in the square in front of St Sofia's Cathedral in Kiev, the cathedral of the Ukrainian breakaway Orthodox Church. At the same time 144,000 of the cult's followers would commit suicide, then three days after the crucifixion they and Maria would be resurrected. It seemed that they believed that the world would end at this time and, as usual, that only they would be saved.

The group had grown over the previous two or three years, and with a successful publicity campaign based on flyposting and the striking looks of Maria Devi, a political opposition to the Ukrainian authorities who were blamed for social breakdown and insufficient food and money, and the development of small communes of believers, it achieved some success. The local and national media seems to have been taken in by some of the propaganda, followed, of course, by the rest of the world. Active believers probably numbered 1,000 at most, rather than the 144,000 who were supposed to be saved, and wild accusations were made about the use of mind-bending drugs. If you know anything about cults, you'll know that when you can depend on poor diet, limited and broken sleep, endless sermonising and study, and separation from the outside world, you just don't need drugs to control people. These simple truths have been practised by the major religions for thousands of years, and perfected in religious orders of all kinds.

On 10 November 1993, the day before the promised crucifixion, and amid vast publicity, about 50 cult members inveigled their way into St Sofia's, and essentially behaved like vandals. They were arrested, as were 500 or so others, and by chance the two cult leaders were picked up as well. In prison, Maria and Yuri were only identified when the Police spotted their followers kissing their feet, but they went on to move doomsday back to November 24. Maria is reported as going on to declare to the Police that: "My name is God. You will remember me forever. The dangerous God will come – nobody knows the day or the time. Because you insult God's name you will fall into the Second Circle of Hell."

November 24 was another serious miss. The last reports of the cult that I've seen sadly record that its hungry, desolate and disappointed cult members were being deprogrammed and reconverted by representatives of a variety of other, socially more respectable cults and religions. Dependency culture indeed.

Aum Supreme Truth

As I write the trial of Shoko Asahara, the leader of the Aum Supreme Truth cult, is in progress in Japan. It may not be over by the time you read this book. What finally brought the cult and its remarkable leader to world prominence was the nerve gas attack on unwitting commuters in the Tokyo subway on 20 March 1995, which left 12 dead and around 5,000 made sick by the gas. There's no telling how the court case will turn out, but the cult itself is one of two recent examples of how belief in the end of the world can lead to violent and sickening behaviour, justified by the cult's members as being an important part of the End Times events that must happen. For cults like Aum the end of the world can't be left for God to arrange – they take an active role in making it happen, and believing it is coming very soon.

Aum is a real doomsday cult, and its members carry on with their beliefs despite the court case. Around 1990, they had believed Asahara when he prophesied to them that Mount Fuji would blow up, and that only he could save the world. Now, they are sure that the end of civilisation as we know it will begin with a frightful war between Japan and America in 1997, that Japan will emerge from this Armageddon as the only world power, and that the members of Aum will then be the most powerful people in the world. Asahara pronounced himself the "Holy Monk Emperor" to be, who would rule while his followers created a post-nuclear utopia. He also spoke of astral journeys, and journeys into space, and of preparing materials and facilities to assist these

Cult members lived lives of often miserable physical and psychological deprivation, and gave both their belongings and their partners to the cult leader. Rumour has it – but then rumour often does – that his followers drank his blood, and made potions from cuttings from his beard, or from his dirty bathwater (well, there wouldn't have been much point making them from his clean bathwater, would there?)

But the cult didn't stop there. Like so many others, it looks as if the children of followers were abused, and that Asahara exploited female cult members. That isn't acceptable, but it isn't uncommon. What is rare is that the cult built up massive stocks of weapons of various kinds and the means to manufacture many more. Gradually, it reached the extreme psychological state of using the lethal poison sarin – a pesticide – first to kill seven people in the city of Matsumoto in June 1994, and later to launch the attack on the Tokyo subway. There is much left to understand about Aum Shinrikyo, and it is only speculation to suggest that they were willing to try to find suitable ways to encourage the foreign aggression and final conflict they believed to be necessary before they became, effectively, the rulers of the world. This might be seen as a peculiarly Japanese cult, that fitted well in a civilisation traditionally both militaristic and nihilistic, having a low regard for the rights and preferences of the individual, but I wouldn't be surprised to see similar cults functioning elsewhere.

The Order of the Solar Temple

Suicide as well as murder drew the world's attention to what turned out to be the Order of the Solar Temple, a cult based in Canada and Switzerland. This group of educated, generally affluent people was led by Joseph di Mambro and Luc Jouret, and they had developed the idea that their destiny lay on Sirius, the brightest star in the sky in the Northern Hemisphere.

Sirius is a popular object of metaphysical speculation, partly because of the account by Robert Temple of the knowledge of the primitive Dogon tribe, who may just have known about a companion "Sirius B", without the astronomical technology to enable them to do so. There is a popular notion that various forms of communicating aliens come from Sirius. Sirius is, in reality, a very hot star and not a habitable planet, but that doesn't seem to trouble the true believers. Hello to the asbestos aliens, the oven-glove people.

There is seldom much point in looking for logical reasons for decisions of this kind. Sirius was where the members of the Order of the Solar Temple wanted to go, and to get there 53 of them died by fire, more or less by choice, in Quebec and Switzerland in October 1994. They believed that the fire was part of the process of transition. Sadly, in addition to dying by fire, they had also became convinced that in a murderous parody of the Biblical end times scenario they should kill the Antichrist before they left. In one of the saddest endings to any young life, they chose a baby of three months for their victim, stabbed his parents to death, killed the child with a stake through his heart, and set fire to their home. The most off-beat and apparently intelligent cult can suddenly turn lethal, for the strangest and slightest of reasons.

Chapter 10

DISSENTERS

Before we start weighing up the real significance of all the Millennial prophecies that haven't gone wrong, it may come as a relief to know that more than half the world really isn't worried about the End Times. Or no more worried than usual, anyway. Somehow, of all the world's major religions only Christianity, the religion of Europe, the New World, and a few other areas of influence, has provided the background of belief and expectation that encourages mass anxiety about the immediate future; certainly it is Christian culture, with its tradition of contact through visits and visions, that all the countries with strong millennial beliefs have in common. And, of course, many cultures and faiths don't share our calendar. The year 2000 really is an important issue: if in your country, or your faith, the date is something else entirely then it just doesn't have the same effect.

Social conditions alone aren't sufficient to lead people to believe in an imminent apocalypse. If that was the case, then some of the states and countries from the former Soviet Union would surely be at the edge of the abyss, waiting for intervention by some great good, or great evil being. There are millions of people who have seen the order of their lives crumble in the past few years. Interpersonal crime that was relatively rare under Communism has not only become common, but has links with organised crime, the exploitation of the masses for the advantage of the few.

In the USA, that kind of exploitation and self-enrichment leads to accusations of Freemasonry, of membership of the Illuminati, of being part of a massive plan by the few against the many. In Russia and other states that once made up the Soviet Union, organised crime is seen for what it is, and the people show every sign of wanting to deal with it by giving more power to the central government, not by dispersing it into groups of patriots and militias. Even where evangelists have gone out to these countries, they have been met with general tolerance rather than mass conversion. Yes, there are successful new age practitioners, but they seem to work more on the level of healing and self-improvement, rather than involving the Russians in the wonderful world of channelling, ascension and Light Workers. Similarly, the horrors of Bosnia haven't led to any new religious movements or beliefs of any significance. The only non human intelligence-type phenomena I have come across there have been the Visions of the Virgin Mary at Medjugorje, but even they were underway before the conflicts began, and have occurred in recognisably Catholic communities.

In my admittedly slightly unusual experience, I've found that if religions have just one particular purpose, it's to enable people to deal with the problems presented by death. Not just with the moment of dying, but with the facts of bereavement, and coping with the absence of someone we wish wasn't absent. Death presents its greatest challenge when it's seen as a point of transition between life here and life somewhere else. What happens to our consciousness when we die? Are we aware of our own death? And if we do go on in some way, where do we go? You only need to look at the amount of interest generated by the very thin evidence offered for the objective reality of the Near-Death Experience to realise how anxious many of us are about the nature of dying, and our destination when we're dead. Not surprisingly, virtually every major world religion, and most of the others, too, have a pretty clear policy on what happens at death. We look to them to tell us how we will be judged when that moment comes, and to what delightful or disgusting place our eternal souls will be committed to when that judgment has been made.

You'll know, now, that these are all standard components of many of our End Times scenarios, although most of the ones we're considering are given interest and edge by the simple threat that they'll happen very soon. The major religions don't usually promise that sort of immediacy, but we should have some idea of what they have to say about the ways we'll meet our Makers, if only to help us understand the background against which the wilder and stranger beliefs have come about.

Zoroastrianism

Zoroastrianism, the ancient faith of Zarathustra, has been hugely influential in the development of other religions – influential to an extent that I ought to explore further, but which I don't have room for here. I can't promise you that, particularly if you believe in the Christian God, the exploration will do anything to help your belief. But facts are facts.

As far as we know, Zoroastrianism was the first major religion to paint a clear picture of the prospects for both the individual after death, and the end of the world in general. Dates are very vague, this may well have happened more than 3,000 years ago, although as in most faiths, ideas and prophecies developed as the years passed by. For the individual, Zoroaster himself would meet the soul of the newly-dead at the Chinvat Bridge. A record of good and evil deeds is considered and depending on the balance between them the soul will make its way to a marvellous paradise or, because of its own troubled conscience, it will be unable to go beyond the bridge, and will live on, alone in "the House of the Lie". This concept of a "personal hell" seems remarkably sophisticated for such an early time; much more real, for instance, than the widely publicised hell seen by the child visionaries at Fatima.

The Zoroastrian End Times scenario is consistent with its belief that there is a constant struggle between Good (Ahuramazd) and Evil (Ahriman); there will be one last great battle, good will triumph, and there will be a general resurrection of humanity. The wicked will suffer horribly for three days, but after that time of purification the whole of humanity will live happily together. There is a broad acceptance that these concepts of judgment, suffering, resurrection, purging or purification, and endless life thereafter weighed heavily in the development of Judaism and Islam, and later in Christianity.

Judaism

It should always be remembered that most of the people who wrote the whole of the Christian Bible were Jews. And if they weren't Jews when they wrote their contributions, they had usually been Jewish previously, or at least had been raised in Jewish culture. The Old Testament and most of the Apocrypha were almost entirely written before the birth of Christ, yet their eschatologies have become Christian ones. In fact, the ideas of life after death, of judgment and of resurrection developed substantially over hundreds of years. There was no clear definition of heaven or hell, no specific element of the body or personality that survived death, and if God was expected to intervene on behalf of His chosen people it was to assist them in battle, in freeing them from slavery, and ensuring them a safe and comfortable life here on earth.

It probably wasn't till the last hundred years BC that ideas of personal survival of death, and of some sort of neutral resting place till a physical resurrection began to appear. Here some of the ideas that we find in the current Fundamentalist End Times scenarios first emerged; for instance, the idea of the Millennium as a period of 1,000 years of God's Kingdom on Earth comes up in the first century AD in the second book of Enoch, at around the same time as other apocalyptic accounts of the kind appear in the Book of Revelation. However, I'm not aware of any particular End Times expectation in mainstream Judaism. In spite of the struggles for the existence and security of the State of Israel, and the way the events involving it are interpreted by all kinds of prophets as having great End Times significance, those specualations are largely Christian affairs, particularly for those who try to spot the Signs of the Times.

Islam

Attempting to make simplistic explanations of Islamic beliefs is a waste of time. It is a faith with one God, Allah, one principal prophet, Muhammad, and one outstanding holy book, the Qur'an. But any faith so massive and widespread has believers and beliefs within it who hold a wide range of views, and face vastly different trials and challenges in maintaining their beliefs. Anyone who has seen the treatment of the Muslims in the former Yugoslavia, or of some groups of Muslims in, say, Iraq, will realise that this is a faith that faces persecution now as it always has faced persecution, with beliefs in personal and world eschatologies that reflect what the faithful have been through.

Broadly, in Islam there is both a personal survival of death, and a clear End Times scenario. After death there are different prospects for believers and unbelievers, the status of each also relating to the individual's conduct in their human life, on the basis that a proper belief entails proper conduct. For the world at large there is a general prospect of resurrection, which follows a reasonably familiar sequence of events involving the appearance of an Antichrist, the return of Christ after 40 days of the reign of the Antichrist, to set up a Kingdom on earth, and then the arrival of a figure who is perhaps Muhammad himself, a judgment, and different destinies, along the lines of heaven and hell, for humanity. But, again, there appears to be no visible speculation as to the identity of the Antichrist, and no expectation of any of these events taking place in the foreseeable future.

Buddhism and Hinduism

Any faith based on the principle of reincarnation, the cycle of birth, death and rebirth, working gradually towards specific personal goals, has little in common with any of our End Times scenarios. In neither of

these great world religions is there any suggestion of massive intervention in human affairs by any external power or intelligence. Yes,
humans are judged, and to a degree rewarded, or punished, accordingly. But these processes are essentially continuous ones, and there is
no expectation sort of a dramatic, world-shaking change in the Earth
and its inhabitants at the coming Millennium or, it seems at any other
time. It may seem odd that both Buddhism and Hinduism have had a
considerable influence on new age beliefs and philosophies, which
often include all kinds of alien and unworldly intelligence that appear
to have no place in either faith. By now, however, you really shouldn't
be expecting logic in what people choose to believe and hope for!

Christianity

You won't be greatly surprised to hear that many Christians, particularly the more liberal and careful ones, have little time for End Times predictions and promises. You may remember the controversies that surrounded important Christians like the Bishop of Durham when they
expressed doubts about the reality of Christ's resurrection from the
dead, about the Virgin Birth, about the Ascension into Heaven. The
same sort of Christians probably have even less time for the Book of
Revelation, regarding it as symbolic at best, and confused and confusing to the ordinary Christian. There are many different degrees of faith
in the specific accuracy of the Bible, and End Times events are one of
the key areas for doubt. To put it another way, if a moderate Christian
is going to decide not to believe in something in the Bible, it may well
be Revelation, Daniel, the Rapture in Thessalonians, and the rest of the
amazing sequence of events that has been developed from the apocalyptic literature. When I write about beliefs and prophecies about the
End of the World, they almost always come from Fundamentalist
Christianity: those who accept every word of the Bible as the absolute
truth, the Word of God.

The "For God's Sake Don't Give A Date" movement

Religious groups and leaders of all varieties have learned a lot about
how to deal with the media, and how not to make themselves look
more foolish than they have to. A prophet should be cautious, and most
aren't! Once an individual or a group becomes convinced that they
have the secret, the answer, the news that everybody has been waiting

for, caution goes to the wind.

But recent years have seen some changes, and not just among the Jehovah's Witnesses, the most public prophets of the past 50 years. After giving specific years for the Second Coming, and ending up with embarrassing failures, they now have a clear policy of avoiding dates altogether. The sequence of events is still predicted in detail, but with no time frame around them.

The Jehovah's Witnesses have little connection with other millennial groups, but the mainstream of Fundamentalism is beginning to catch on to the problems that being wrong can cause, but the way they go about it seems to me a little odd. The Bible has long been considered capable of interpretation, given sufficient "prayerful understanding", and one of the areas that could be understood was meant to be when the various signs of the end times were all in place. No, the Bible does not actually give dates, but what about the "date verses" from the Book of Daniel? Do they suddenly have no meaning? Aren't they part of the Word of God, too?

So, this is quite a dramatic turn about, but it's certainly receiving publicity as I write. In the May 1996 issue of the magazine *Renewal*, a very professional British Christian monthly, there's a feature titled, "Christ's glorious return: in God's way, in God's time". Richard Foster, a pastor from Colorado, doesn't only take the line that: "There simply is no countdown to Armageddon. The future is contingent upon the give-and-take of God's initiative and our response. Faith not some artificial calendar scheme, is the catalyst for divine providence." No, he goes beyond that, and mocks several different groups of believers whose prophecies have failed, and whose hopes have been dashed. He even summarises the sincere and Christian, in all the best senses of the word, William Miller, in a few dismissive words, and includes Harold Camping and Hal Lindsey in his criticisms.

In politics, this would be the work of the "spin doctors", using PR tactics and the facilities of the media to make a story look like you want it to look. And I think that politics are at work here, for the very reason that there is a growing "millennium consensus", that all sorts of prophecies are being made, but that many of the wealthy and established elements of the Fundamentalist movement don't want to risk the comfortable positions they have achieved on account of taking the Bible too seriously. A couple of months ago an important book arrived in the UK's major religious bookshops from the USA. Written by two professors from the influential Moody Bible Institute, it is called *Doomsday Delusions – What's Wrong with Predictions About the End of the World*. It expends 30 pages on explaining how wrong poor old William Miller and his followers turned out to be, and a great many more making a comprehensive case for being so careful about the end of the world as to say nothing at all in case it turns out to be wrong.

If you want a quick author's prophecy here, it's that we'll see a good deal more "don't give a date" propaganda between now and the Millennium. Personally, I don't mind what people prophesy about or believe in, so long as they're honest about it. In the middle of a book that collects together more End Times prophecies than you've ever seen in one place before, I have to point out that there are millions of people all over the world who really don't care about the approach of the year 2000, and a good many who, having different calendars to ours, don't even know. But people who do know, and do care, and then pretend that they don't, that's a different matter entirely.

Chapter 11

THE BEGINNING OF THE NEW AGE

There are visions of a dramatically new and different world that don't involve either the Second Coming of Jesus Christ, or the landing of the flying saucers. I might describe the New Age way of thinking as one in which nothing is impossible. This principle underlies beliefs that humanity has no limits, that consciousness has no limits, and that if we look upward and inward instead of being bound by the demands of our bodies, and the dismal world we live in, we can progress to a level of spiritual awareness and existence we never dreamed could be possible.

Now, I'll admit from the outset that while I'm more than happy with spiritual awareness and development, and I hope humanity will move in some of the positive directions the New Age movement suggests, I'm very unimpressed with the way that movement functions. You may remember from encountering Chaucer at school how Indulgences and Pardons were sold by representatives of the Catholic Church, to ensure that the purchasers did not go to Hell for their sins; or that their time in Purgatory was minimised or, indeed, that they would go straight to Heaven. The sale of these sorts of promises and guarantees was one of the great issues raised by Martin Luther, and it had left many Catholics deeply disillusioned with their Church, if not their faith.

Without wishing to labour the issue, that's rather how I see much of the New Age movement. You can buy all kinds of spirituality and salvation, and some sorts will cost you very dear indeed. There is no more evidence that they will work here and now than there was for the indulgences and pardons of the European Middle Ages.

Happily, not all New Age wisdom is so expensive, and there is a wealth of material in books, magazines, cassettes and the occasional video which will bring you into contact with non-human intelligences from all over the known and unknown universe, from our dimension and many others, from our time as well as the past and future.

You've probably heard of channelling, which is the description usually applied to human beings producing verbal or written communications, the content of which has come from other, non-human intelligences. It's a fairly close relative of Spiritualist mediumship, except that it doesn't present the problem of living relatives expecting accurate and verifiable information to be passed on by the communicator. It's a closer relative of much religious experience, where messages from identifiable, traditional figures are received. The content is very similar to what the Space Brothers told those who met them on lonely desert roads in the fifties. Intriguingly, much of it is meant to come from the same inhabited areas of the universe where the alien abductors live, but this can be confusing. It is seldom that either group refers to the other, and they certainly don't share a common philosophy.

But the channellers are many, and their messages are surprisingly consistent in their promises of our increased spirituality, and the care and concern of a host of amazing entities and intelligences. The heightening of our spiritual awareness, the process of linking and communicating with higher entities and life-forms so that we might function without reference to our physical bodies is commonly called Ascension. And it isn't just spiritual and individual. When presented as something to be achieved by humanity in substantial numbers – "becoming a Galactic Human" – it's a full-on "End of the World as we Know It" event, often said to be accompanied, or preceded by, dramatic Earth changes of the polar shift and earthquake variety. There is a definite salvation element to many of the predictions and promises that are made – some will have to suffer, some or many will be left behind, only the chosen are certain of the Ascension.

Being chosen seems to be a matter of individual choice, and it isn't hard to identify yourself as a channeller, a light being or a starchild. Some have their own unique communicators, others share theirs with others. Ashtar, Sananda and the Archangel Michael are particular favourites at present, and seem to communicate through many human channels. Ancient non-Christian gods and goddesses make contact, too. The ancient Egyptian deity Thoth, for instance, communicates through Alton, the editor of the fascinating Australian magazine *Eagle's Wings*. Alton is also known as Brian – it's not uncommon for the channellers to take on more appropriate names than the ones they're accustomed to when they start channelling. He belongs to the "Alpha Omega order of Melchizedek".

Thoth spoke about imminent changes late in 1995, explaining the dramatic effects of the "merkaba", an energy field that is, apparently, impervious to negative or dark energies, and is now in place around the Earth

"Once locked into Mother Earth you then need to honour the presence of the cosmic Christ by encoding your merkaba energy field into the newly formed Christ consciousness grid. This immediately will draw the attention of Lord Sananda and the ascended masters. At that point a clarion call is heard around the universe that another soul is ready to enter the kingdom of heaven…

"Linear time is no longer a reality. You now are living in a special time where all things exist and create simultaneously. Understand what you can create now. All the tools for Ascension are with you. The mystery schools of the past are now collectively reborn to encompass the Earth. Indeed the whole of your dear Mother Earth is now your sacred mystery school and you are the 'star' pupils."

Thoth's message – a mixture of scientific concepts we do not understand, assertions of the great future of the Earth, and of the special role in the Ascension for those with whom he communicates – is a good example of what the channelling entities have to say. And there are so many of them saying it, too. Just looking at a few recent issues of the Australian magazines *Eagle's Wings*, *The Earth Star and Starchild*, and *Connecting Link* from the USA (don't believe that everything New Age happens in California – I have the impression that it's really Australia out there on the leading edge), I found that all the following non-human intelligences had been in touch in the last year or so:

The Three (Dolphins), Archangel Michael, the God Source, Theodore (a mid-causal plane entity), the White Brotherhood, Ascended Masters St Germain and Djwhal Khul, White Crow, Adama (Ascended Master and High Priest of Telos, a subterranean city beneath Mt Shasta in California), the Cetaceans (I think that's dolphins again), Ashtar, Lord Sananda, the Cassiopaeans (sixth density beings of light), Commander Apollo of the starship The Golden Crysolis ("Universe 45 of the Ashtar Celestial Zone"), which is always in contact with the Delos Command and the Eagelian Triad, Tobias from the Elemental Kingdom, Ascended Masters Babaji and Sanat Kumara, P'taah, The Arcturians, the Integration and Test Team of the Ashtar Command, Elvis Aaron Presley, Ascended Master Kuthumi, Master Korton, The Elohim in conjunction with the Time Lords and the Law Lords, Lady Nada, Thoth himself, the Ashtar Command of the Galactic Federation, Commander Akas of Starfleet, Agartha of the Underground Claims (the first time he had spoken with those above ground since Lemurian times), Essetron, Jesus Christ Sananda, Mother Kwan Yin – Goddess of Mercy, Adonai, ZaKaiRan and Vastika (emissaries from the Earth Ascension Alliance), the Mothership Starbase, and the Interdimensional Visionary Masters. I could go on. Just bear in mind that all of these entities have both know about, and expect to play a part in, the future of us all.

A particularly clear statement of the future can be found in the book *Advent Calendar for the Salvation of the Planet Earth*. The original name of the author appears to have been Linda J Joslin, but she channels as Demara, and the book's teachings apparently came primarily from the Archangel Raphael, with contributions from the Archangel Gabriel, Archangel Uriel, Archangel Michael, Master Kathumi and Master Hilarion. A powerful team of non-human intelligences. So much so that the publisher explains that "this book carries an energy which activates the codes within us. We have been at pains not to change the meaning by the usual editing process... We have the privilege of being incarnate at the time of transition of the whole planet from a Third dimension environment to a Fifth... It seems that we are in the time of the Revelation of St John – of the Apocalypse – a time to be judged. The Advent Calendar is addressed to humanity and offers very practical suggestions of how we, as individuals and groups, can begin to change rigid minds and our materialistic lifestyles, our relationships with one another, and open up to the infinite." There is a lot about cleansing, a lot about the drowning of land and, no doubt, of people. "The Spring Cleaning of the Planet Earth" will clearly be unpleasant, and it seems that believing is as necessary to personal salvation in this scenario as it is in most traditional religions.

Sadly, the combined wisdom of four Archangels and two Ascended Masters, who apparently also reassembled most of the "White Brotherhood", is not concentrated on the issues that many of us, given three wishes perhaps, might wish to sort out. For all the talk of healing there is nothing about finding cures for cancer or AIDS. For all the claims of involvement in the cleansing and rebalancing of the Earth, we are not told how to produce dependable foods in barren countries, or how to ensure that, simplest of wishes, so many people don't go to sleep hungry every night. This book is just an example of many, if not all, of its kind. I can't say that it means that the predictions for our immediate future are wrong, but I'm not struck by the kindness of Archangels, Ascended Masters or the White Brotherhood.

The New Age movement isn't really one coherent whole. It shares certain books and icons, but there's a multitude of gurus to follow, meditation techniques to learn, learning techniques to learn, workshops to attend, books to read. As I write, the adverts are full of Reiki and Neuro-Linguistic Programming (NLP), but in a couple of years there will be different fashions. There are plenty of activities to keep New Agers busy, experiencing new ways of singing, dancing, reading, breathing, sleeping, or achieving altered states of consciousness. And the opportunities to become a guru and spiritual teacher yourself are unprecedented – you can easily be one of those running the courses and workshops, teaching Reiki and NLP, past-life regression and the rest. A key element of sharing any truth or half-truth with your followers is to promise either that they will themselves be dramatically improved and changed, or that they will have an important part to play in some version of the Ascension, the dramatic changes in the Earth's spirituality.

You'll find some peculiar quirks among the more spiritual New Age beliefs. Fear of an imminent New World Order is common, along with paranoia about the intentions of a variety of national governments, and the notions of cover-up and mind control. The anti-tax, anti-central government attitudes of the US survivalist and patriot tendencies appear from time to time. There are people believing in more gods than ever, but the evidence so far is that these gods care about us no more than their ancient predecessors. The New Age believers in those gods are expecting changes every bit as immediate, and dramatic, and generally deadly, as the most right-wing Christian fundamentalist. Fortunately, the expectations are so dramatically different that it isn't possible that both will turn out to be correct.

Chapter 12

THE BIBLE, AND THE NEW WORLD ORDER

This book isn't meant to be the "Bumper Book of Crackpots", and I don't intend to start writing that undesirable tome now. But I think it's important to understand how ideas and beliefs from different millennial sources can be brought together by a person or a group, and how easily the resulting creed, however strange, can attract eager followers. With a little research you can find a lot more groups and individuals with beliefs like these, but here's just three examples: one very public prophet from each side of the Atlantic, and a shadowy group based in Australia and Germany. All have something serious and prophetic to say about the next few years, and all make me feel uneasy.

Texe Marrs

A charismatic, forceful individual is often much more important than the ideas he comes up with, and charisma and a new, exciting message can usually guarantee success in most areas of prophecy. Texe Marrs is an awesome American evangelist who operates Living Truth Ministries from Austin, Texas. He is regarded by more mainstream evangelists and church leaders as a maverick, and by more liberal commentators as somebody with a quite remarkable view of reality.

Yet his views, which derive from a totally fundamentalist view of the Bible in which every word is literally true, either influence or reflect the fear and paranoia thinking that pervades much of the new age movement. Marrs would probably be horrified by this thought, but I've been reading *Flashpoint – A Newsletter Ministry of Texe Marrs* for three years now, and listening to some of his audio cassettes. He also publishes books and videos. His views are particularly close to those who live in fear of the New World Order. He is as stern a critic as you'll find of Freemasonry and the Illuminati, and believes that a NWO agenda underpinned the earliest years of the US constitution:

"In other words, our Masonic forefathers masterfully tricked the citizenry into believing a lie – that the government would forever guarantee the rights of free citizens. In fact, these men made sure that dictatorial, ungodly, and savage breaches and violations could craftily be written later into law simply by the ruse of treaties."

Personally, I've always believed in the "cock-up" theory of government. If any government has a viable plan that covers more than a couple of years ahead, then there's never been much evidence for it. I have the impression that most governments decide what to do after events have occurred, usually in a state of uninformed panic. As you'll realise, my beliefs don't really fit comfortably with those who see a massive, ancient conspiracy devoted to controlling mankind and defying the will of God, and there are plenty of people out there who'd disagree with me. Texe Marrs sees Satan's legions coming "disguised as the scary "grays" or the friendly "Pleidians". He said that the 1994 Biological Diversity Treaty was drafted by the "world's slimiest occultists", organised by an "Illuminati baron". That "agents of the Rockefellers and the Rothschilds are working behind the scenes to bring about a World Empire headquartered in Jerusalem." Seeing the present and a future Pope involved in this, he asks: "Will the Pope's plans culminate in a mutually enriching, global Masonic dictatorship?"

Yet he also publicises the writing and thinking of new age/conspiracy theorists like Jim Keith, who you might imagine would engender fear and distrust in the heart of a Fundamentalist Christian like Marrs. Advertising Keith's book, *Black Helicopters Over America – Strikeforce for the New World Order*, Marrs asks what is the meaning of hundreds of unmarked Black Helicopter sightings throughout the United States? Why are foreign troops secretly moving war equipment across America? Are emergency detention centres being set up to house potentially subversive American citizens?

Marrs comes up with specific predictions too, although his version of the coming Earth changes is an utterly depressing one in which, oddly, God seems to play little part. Writing in 1995, he predicted that by 2000 AD, a "brutal worldwide campaign of tyranny, deception, manipulation, torture, mass murder and dictatorial control" would have enabled "the elitists to firmly maintain complete, Big Brother dominance of the masses". He sees gun control and the "environmental, Mother Earth movement" as part of the conspiracy, and touches base with the survivalists in asking why concentration camps are being built, and whether "Christians and patriots" can "stop this monstrous plot".

He sees the FBI behind the Oklahoma bomb, Bill Clinton as wanting "to turn America's public schools into occult, black magic laboratories", asks whether "Ross Perot is an undercover agent assigned a major role in the New World Order conspiracy", and suspects that the Mary of the Roman Catholic Church is not the real Mary of the Bible, but the "Mary of Satan". Marrs can fear anything and anybody, but claims that his God will, eventually, defeat all these strange and often unlikely opponents. These are just the ideas of one man and his ministry, but the ideas stretch into all kinds of movements and groups. At the heart of them is the belief in a conspiracy of the rich and powerful against the rest of us, and the fear of the imposition of this mysterious New World Order.

David Icke

David Icke is Britain's own New Age prophet, an intelligent man with previous roles as a professional footballer, and as a convincing spokesman for the Green Party. He is a very effective communicator, but the value of what he chooses to communicate is the subject of some argument.

Like so many New Age writers, he picks material more or less randomly from a huge range of sources to make what could be an interesting case. His underlying theory is that we, the people, are being and always have been seriously conspired against by those in power. That whoever we think we have democratically chosen to lead us, or shape our world, what we end up with is what is chosen for us by some gigantic, ancient conspiracy. He characterises the conspirators as the Illuminati, that powerful combination of freemasons, politicians, church leaders, scientists, bankers and others, who have known for thousands for years that there are "long-established links between Earth-bound humanity and beings from other dimensions and planets in the Universe", but this knowledge has been ruthlessly suppressed. He depicts the Freemasons as run by the Vatican, and the world run by named groups and specific families, who often attend great conferences at which our fate is regularly revised. You can find the same names and titles in so many different books about the conspiracies against us – those who write them have even earned the name "conspiracy theorists".

But among the usual unsupported assertions about the Rothschilds and the Rockefellers, the International Monetary Fund and the World Bank, the Council on Foreign Relations, the Trilateral Commission, the Club of Rome, the Bilderberg Group, the Royal Institute of International Affairs and the United Nations, one thoroughly nasty piece of material was presented by Icke in his well-publicised 1994 book, *The Robots' Rebellion – The Story of the Spiritual Renaissance*.

The sheer extent of Icke's blunder – at least, I really hope it's a blunder, and not a deliberate presentation of anti-Jewish propaganda – leaves me with no confidence whatever in his commitment to research, or his grasp of reality. Considering the almost total lack of proof for most of what he says, he simply seems to have succeeded in distilling the ignorance of many years of groundless speculation. He expresses no doubts in claiming that, "In the 1800s some documents surfaced called the Protocols of the Wise Men of Zion. Almost everything these documents proposed to do has happened in this century."

Icke's interpretation of history has an organisation he calls The Brotherhood having dominated world events for more than 6,000 years, "since Sumer and Egypt." He sees the Protocols as "such an excellent indication of the Brotherhood's intentions that I will use passages from them through the book". In a slight concession to not appearing too anti-Jewish, too anti-Semitic, he renames them the Illuminati Protocols, but retains the use of the Yiddish word goyim, which can be used collectively to refer to non-Jews, as a term for those who are to be manipulated. He quotes repeatedly from the renamed Illuminati Protocols, using introductions like, "Or as the Illuminati Protocols put it in the 1800s". Indeed, it's just about all that he quotes from, because there is no tangible, testable evidence for any Illuminati conspiracy. Rather like the prophecies of Nostradamus, or the interpretation of the meaning of the passages in the Great Pyramid, you can simply make up stuff about the Illuminati without any great danger of being found out.

I'm not going to reprint the contents of these wretched documents, but this is as good a place as any to publish the known facts about one of the foundations stones of the conspiracy theorists, and of those who tell us to be afraid of the New World Order. Robin Ramsay is the editor of *Lobster*, the magazine that deals with all kinds of parapolitics and conspiracies. He puts the facts bluntly as he comments on a description of the Protocols as "the apparently faked documents used to stir up hatred against the Jews earlier this century". He says:

"The full title, at least the full title on the first English translation in the 1920s, was *The Protocols of the Meetings of the Learned Elders of Zion*. And there's no "apparently faked" about it. *The Protocols* are a piece of psy-war material from the early 20th century, initially circulated by the Czar's secret police, and translated into English by a journalist called Victor Marsden. Everything about *The Protocols'* genesis, authorship and circulation is known. It's the fakest of fakes; the crappiest UFO magazine is more plausible."

Every time I see a pronouncement by Icke, I think of *The Protocols.* They aren't about the evil done by the Illuminati. They were made up to persuade the ignorant and the bigoted of the evil done, and planned, by a supposed international Jewish conspiracy. Sadly, those intentions are still being fulfilled. Some modern American bigots have suggested that although they were written later than has been pretended, they still contain the truth, discreetly covered up. But they, too, would have no trouble establishing what lies they are. It seems that they just don't want to.

QDW – Australia

Some strange stuff is coming out of Australia, none stranger than the propaganda put out by the "QDW Australia Association", which seems to operate at several extremes, and which I find distinctly worrying. They've managed to place adverts in a number of UK newsstand magazines, and I suspect they're doing the same elsewhere.

On the surface, theirs are the wildest of wild claims, but after a while the clues begin to appear:

"We as Atlanteans, the remaining few of the original white race of Atlantis, not only survived the downfall of Atlantis, and also the decline of the Egyptian Empire, but we survived during our continuing reincarnation cycle the persecution and inquisition of the Christian Church. But we have to face another enemy who is not known by many people, the New World Order comprising of one Ruler, One God, One Hierarchy and One Doctrine...

"We as the reincarnated Atlanteans (from Sirius, Orion) have one chance to combine our power, protect our tribes, seal our knowledge against foreign intruders, celebrate our most sacred rituals to reopen the door into our real home across the universe...

"We know that the Grey Hospital in Arizona, USA, where all the abducted ones are delivered to, was built by Atlanteans who are still among us today, living in human bodies... Their UFOs are not æroplanes from beyond the frequency border. They are built here on Earth (during the Atlantean Era) they have their airport here on Earth

(Arizona, USA)."

The clues, for those of you unaccustomed to these things, are the appearance in just one of many booklets and leaflets, of the words "white race", "protect our tribes", "foreign intruders", "persecution" and "inquisition". Dig a little further, and you'll find educational courses dealing with "ancient pagan culture", "neonazis" and the "migration of nations". You'll find that there's a QDW Sanctuary in Australia, where "for all seminars everybody will wear a similar dress", where tape and video recorders, mobile phones, radios and cameras are forbidden. The QDW magazine is called *Elite*. And yes, QDW also has several branches in Germany.

There have been several suggestions of an unhealthy crossover between neo-fascism and those who claim opposition to the New World Order. Where Texe Marrs approaches the issue from the Fundamentalist angle, the US patriot and survivalist groups from a form of anti-government white supremacism, and David Icke sees fit to refer to the repulsive and fraudulent *Protocols of the Elders of Zion* as if they were more than racist lies, QDW combine a variety of earlier fears and prejudices, and overlay them with abduction paranoia and the mysteries of ancient races. They purvey spells to gain protection from abduction, they sell details of magical rituals, they thrive on fear of other races, different skin colours, interbreeding and impurity, and demand commitment and self-purification. If you don't find these people worrying, the lessons of the past 60 years have been pretty much wasted on you.

Chapter 13

THE BLESSING – HOLY AND UNHOLY SPIRITS

One of my theories, which may not be original, is that when people want and expect dramatic, lasting change, they start communicating directly with their gods. We have all sorts of gods at present, both traditional and new, and we are communicating with them like never before. Not in the old ways, through priests and intermediaries and prayer but directly, through meetings, interventions, journeys and the taking over of our very bodies. Quite apart from the multitude of people lying back and thinking of the Pleiades – accepting the channelled messages of high-powered entities from the beyond – there are two other extremes of this kind of behaviour. We'll consider the reports of abduction by alien beings, but first there's the strange matter of the Toronto Blessing, in which suburban Christianity meets something very like Santería or Voodoo.

It's called the Toronto Blessing because it started in the Vineyard Church at Toronto Airport. Airport churches aren't famous for being well attended, but this has become one of the most famous in the world, as pastors and church leaders from all over the world visit to take this extraordinary experience back to their own churches. But what is it, and why might it be a Blessing?

I've done some research on historical revivals and impassioned religious movements, and certain phenomena are quite common. Speaking in tongues occurs regularly, falling over when hands are laid on a believer by a leader is an already established phenomenon. There is often great excitement, verging on hysteria, and sometimes there is prophecy, and an internal awareness of God's wishes for the individual, or even for the group to which they belong. Mental communication through the mind and the brain, if you like, together with that bit of falling over and the convincingly Biblical incidence of "tongues".

Since the 1970s there have been clear and repeated demands and exhortations for revival, for much the same reasons as those given by the religious visions we've considered. That society is breaking down, and God's intervention is the only way to salvation. And not only is revival – the mass acceptance of basic Biblical truths, and a personal, but usually widespread commitment to live a life completely committed to Jesus Christ – an end in itself. Until these commitments and conversions have taken place, Christ will not return for those He has chosen, and who have chosen Him. Revival isn't just a transformation in human behaviour as dramatic as any of the others we've seen, it's a route to the Second Coming. This is the motive that sends many thousands of committed pastors, evangelists and missionaries out all over the world bringing, as it's sometimes put, the sheep into the fold. I suppose this is why it's called a Blessing.

Revival behaviour has often been at the edge of what is socially acceptable, and groups of believers can become as involved, and as devoted to a charismatic leader, as in any other cult or belief group. The ways people are affected by the events associated with the Toronto Blessing go strikingly further than any recent mass movement. Indeed, it has split the evangelical movement because the extremes of behaviour many see as holy are interpreted by others as the work of Satan. The British just don't behave like this in church. Here's a description in *Alpha* magazine of the behaviour of hundreds of delegates at a Vineyard network conference in Bournemouth:

"Bodies littered the floor during the afternoon 'ministry time' for the Bournemouth delegates. Prayer teams scurried over them like soldier ants to the accompaniment of shrieks, howls and a cry that sounded like an air raid siren.

"Many of those who packed out the town's International Centre appeared to be a mature 40-something, and older. Yet that didn't stop them from falling, shaking or even curling up like a baby... Key members of the Toronto team could be seen hopping over bodies and freely administering the 'laying on of hands' .

"The preaching of evangelist John Arnott was punctuated by howls and cries from a number of the delegates. One woman suddenly jerked in her seat, flung her arm back over her head and howled. As if caught doing something naughty, she put her hand over her mouth and tried to recompose herself."

Another Christian, at the Bookham Baptist Church in Surrey, described his personal experience of what seemed to him like a genuinely external and irresistible force,

"I lasted about three seconds before I found I had to sit down in my chair. I spent the next 15 minutes or so desperately trying to keep upright in the chair, trying not to fall on the floor. All of a sudden it was as if someone had switched on a big electro-magnet and sucked me to the floor. I can't explain why, but I just started laughing; and I went on laughing for about three-quarters of an hour. The only way I can describe it is like when a child is being tickled. I wasn't laughing at anything funny or at anything in particular, it was as if someone was tickling me and I just couldn't stop."

Common as this strange behaviour has become in North America, where it began, and more recently in Britain, the phenomena can follow wherever the message of the Blessing is taken. For instance, when Action Europe was doing its missionary work in Bulgaria:

"Bulgarian pastors experienced a real move of the Holy Spirit at a three day conference we sponsored... As we began to minister, barriers came down and leaders, young and old, really responded to the moving of the Spirit. There was lots of laughter and bodies all over the floor! Afterwards we had to explain the phenomena which were previously unknown there and people went away with a renewed vision for their nation."

Muriel Shelbourne, a respected minister with the Assemblies of God, went to preach at Nairobi Bible College, in Kenya. She encountered phenomena that would be called paranormal in another context, as well as more of the Toronto events. It's remarkable how fine the line can be between one strange experience and another:

"That Sunday night as I started preaching about the river of God flowing I saw a miracle in front of my eyes. I had to take my shoes off because it was holy ground. There were insects all over the ground; there were pit-holes; it was cold and hard, but it was holy ground and I saw those students responding in a way that was incredible. The staff knew of nothing as dramatic happening in the entire 27-year history of the college. Students were on their faces; some were on their backs. The missionaries, their families and little children were all there. Even the principal was impacted. For 45 minutes you couldn't move. You dared not touch it.

"The dean's wife, one of those very distinguished, contained and refined people who wasn't into anything that was off-centre as far as she was concerned, said that as I was standing there holding out my hands asking God the Holy Ghost to come to these people and anoint them with fresh oil, she saw a light shining right around where I was standing. As I was talking about the fire falling and igniting the house, she said she could actually see the light diffusing and these little lights were scattering all over the place landing on the students' heads. When that happened, she said, it was like an explosion and they started either crying or shouting or weeping or groaning and speaking in tongues and all these different demonstrations, responses and manifestations of the Spirit."

The phenomena of the Blessing continue to develop. As I write, the debate is about what have been called "animal noises", and whether these are "Biblical", whether similar events can be found in what was written two or three thousand years ago. If they can, then the Blessing is holy. If they aren't, it may be anything but, just another temptation sent to distract believers from their faith. Good or evil, I personally see Toronto as a perfect movement for the last years of this century. People who wouldn't have dreamed of it 10 years ago believe that they can go to certain churches and meetings where they, personally, will be taken over, filled, overshadowed by a Spirit they see as holy, and who will change their lives, and the course of history. There will be more, and stranger yet, to come.

Chapter 14

HYBRIDS & HIGH STRANGENESS – ABDUCTING OUR FUTURE

There is another, growing group of believers who have become convinced of the most peculiar truth. They accept that they are being taken over and controlled by higher powers, and they believe that they are key players in a plan that will dramatically change not only the future of our world, but of many other worlds, too. Like the New Age believers in channelled entities from distant star systems, like those who go to church to be taken over by an irresistible force that sends them reeling, laughing and grunting to the floor, they are communicating directly with their gods. They have only been doing it for a few years. I suspect they will only be doing it for a few years more.

The ultimate external intervention in our lives must be our capture, assault and imprisonment as we become part of a programme of enforced interbreeding with alien entities. This isn't God coming to judge the good and the bad, as openly declared in the Bible and other religious scriptures. This isn't a spiritual involvement with advanced, caring minds from other worlds and star systems. The alien abduction scenario is an extraordinary part of the Millennium Consensus, which suggests the most far-reaching change in the pattern of human life that I can imagine. The ultimate end of the world as we know it, our own disorganised but comprehensible lives replaced by a future chosen by a whole range of non-human intelligences, in which we apparently fulfil their needs and desires, powerless to fight back, or make our own choices.

The history of alien abductions is complicated but rather short. From 1947 onwards, plenty of people had described the trips they'd taken in flying saucers, in the company of friendly, humanoid spacemen – and occasionally women. But no report of an unconscious, unwilling abduction was made before 1960, and the main flood of reports didn't begin till the 1980s. Plenty of individuals have now, their recall assisted by regression hypnosis and other forms of altered state of consciousness, claimed that they were contacted or abducted as small children back in the forties or fifties. It's strange that not one of them ever said anything about it then.

Thousands of people, many of them educated, reasonably successful, apparently mature and sane, have reported the most intimate encounters with the alien beings that have abducted them. In particular, over recent years they have become sure that they have been abducted because they are a part of a programme of interbreeding with alien beings. They say that they are being used to breed human/alien hybrids, and that they have seen the hybrid babies and children produced as part of this organised programme of interbreeding. More than that the abductees, and many of those who investigate and write about them, claim that they were chosen to be part of this interbreeding programme as babies or very small children. Some claim that they agreed to taking on this task in a time before their birth, or were chosen while in the womb.

You're probably familiar with a lot of the story of abductions. For me, the episodes of *The X-Files* that deal with this subject are the most intriguing, and are often the most successful. For all of the outrageous challenges that abductions make to the consensus reality of the rest of the world, they also have a strong appeal. It is science-fiction come true, but more than that. It that makes those involved feel important and needed, if in a very strange way.

The usual explanation for the interbreeding is based on the need of the aliens to secure genetic input for their race, which is no longer able to reproduce and replenish its racial stock by itself. It is a peculiar suggestion, not scientifically sound, and it has some nasty parallels with Nazi ideas of eugenics, of choosing who breeds with whom to produce some sort of master race, more developed, superior to those who have gone before. If you want a prediction for the future, I'd guess that something like a "master race" concept will emerge from the abductee groups, so that instead of just claiming to be different and misunderstood, they'll also start telling us all that they're better, and chosen, and that we ordinary folk can't understand because we're not capable of doing so.

As well as the core belief that people – mostly women, but certainly not all – are being taken away into alien spacecraft, tested, probed, interfered with, impregnated, aborted, or having bodily fluids and samples extracted for use in some sort of in vitro fertilisation, there's the growing belief about government involvement. There are all sorts of strands to this. At the simple end of the range, there's the assertion of back-engineering by US scientists of the technology of alien craft that crashed in the New Mexico area (Roswell, Socorro, Corona and so on) in 1947-1948. In between, an ongoing co-operation between the US government and aliens that survived one or more of those crashes, to help in the development of space and arms technology. At the extreme, there are the accusations that in return for access to alien technology the US government has agreed to allow the abduction and sexual exploitation by aliens of a specified number of US citizens, and unlimited access to the slaughter and mutilation of cattle and other animals, supposedly also needed by the aliens for their regeneration, or some other purpose beyond our understanding.

Not surprisingly, these beliefs have resulted in allegations of a cover-up by the US government – all very *X-Files* indeed. But as is always the case with cover-ups and conspiracies, the accused just can't win. If there isn't any truth in the stories, then they say there isn't. But they'd say that if they were covering up the truth, too, wouldn't they? Just because somebody doesn't tell you something doesn't mean they have something to tell you!

Recently, some of the major abduction researchers – some names to look out for are John Mack, David Jacobs, Budd Hopkins and Whitley Streiber, but there are plenty more – have started putting a timespan on the abduction phenomenon. There are suggestions that it began in the forties or fifties, or even later, and that it will reach an end, of this stage anyway, in the next 20 years and probably sooner. They also suggest that there are deliberate standards and criteria for the selection of abductees, and that abductions run in families because the aliens like to take three or four successive generations.

These ideas go hand in hand with the belief that there are ever-increasing numbers of specially bred alien/human hybrid children in what can only be described as nurseries in space, to which the human parents are repeatedly taken to see their offspring. They fit with the not uncommon belief that there are "star children" on Earth, who properly belong elsewhere and often become aware that they are not really human. A popular American concept is of the "starseed", and some specialist channellers offer refresher programmes to remind the exiled starseed of what life was like on their home planets in the star systems of the Pleiades, Arcturus or whatever.

Even among the best-selling authors and researchers involved in the abduction business – and never forget how much money a successful book about abductions can make – there is no agreement about the nature of the aliens running these programmes for breeding hybrids. Hopkins and Jacobs see the humans involved as no more than victims. David Jacobs has commented that, "I am pessimistic. The more I learn about this phenomenon, the more I have to reign myself back from falling into despair... the evidence inexorably leads to a pessimistic view of the future. I fear for the future. And I fear for my children... The aliens have an incredibly advanced technology. They can do what they want to do."

Despite its reported brutality, Professor John Mack of Harvard University sees the abduction experience quite differently – as transformational, something which can bring great benefits to humanity. He says that "the human-alien relationship itself evolves into a powerful bond. Despite their resentment and terrorisation, the abductees may feel deep love towards the alien beings." At a recent UFO conference in Sheffield I heard Whitley Streiber, author of the best-selling *Communion*, explain how he saw our future in terms of liaising and working with the aliens. He said: "A lot of people will be left behind, but I think mankind is joining the cosmos." Knowing what persecution and suffering human beings have coped with over the years, it is good that hope can so often overwhelm grim reality.

If, that is, any of this abduction business is real. Any reader of this book, or of *Fortean Times*, should be aware that it is possible for almost anybody to believe in almost anything. Not just to believe in the vague sense that a lot of people say they believe in God, but to believe positively and wholeheartedly in the reality of a personal contact with a non-human intelligence. To have absolute conviction about the message that was given to them by that being, and the importance of their mission to spread that message, regardless of how crazy and unlikely it might sound. Bearing that in mind, let's look at the experiences of the abductees, and see what they have in common with the rest of our prophets and End Times believers.

What they don't often have in common is spontaneous recall. Most visionaries and prophets, or those who have experiences in which prophecies are revealed to them, have a direct and immediate recollection of their experience. However extraordinary or unbelievable what they say they have been through, nobody else has to be involved in bringing that memory out. Yes, there are cases where the original recollection is enhanced or embroidered, but seldom is it changed.

Abductees seldom recall the whole of their experience spontaneously and immediately. Although hypnotic regression is not used in every case, some sort of assistance to recall usually is. It may be another psychological technique, or it may be the use of a witness support group, where those who already recall and believe support others in the process of sharing their experiences. This isn't surprising, because there is a widespread belief that the aliens place a kind of block on the memories of the abduction experience. And there is a belief among many of the investigators, which they do nothing to discourage, that they can use techniques which will lift that alien-imposed block. It's a strange claim, for the truth of which there isn't a shred of evidence, but it is common for a would-be abductee to go to an investigator with a memory of no more than a bright light and 20 minutes of a journey that they can't recall, and after a session or two of hypnosis to produce recollections of the most complex and frightening abductions.

My own suspicion is that the way in which people are assisted in recalling abduction memories is far too close for safety to the methods used by therapists accused of encouraging the incidence of False Memory Syndrome. On occasions, this has led to the person in therapy "recalling" utterly false "memories" of being abused as a child, when the remembered abuse could not have taken place. But apart from the method of establishing the memories, true or false, there is much in common between abductees and those who have experiences that lead them to prophesy.

In a recent article in *Fortean Times* I speculated as to whether the people now claiming to have been abducted might be the same as went into monasteries and convents a hundred years ago and more, and still do in countries where abductions never seem to happen. The description of nuns as the "Brides of Christ" reminded me particularly of the relationship many female abductees seem to have developed with their abductors. These people gained the security of a separate, distinct community, based on a relationship with non-human intelligences not shared by most of humanity, an authoritarian command structure offering them support and confirmation for their beliefs and experiences, and the likelihood of approval if those experiences continued. For the abductees, the command structure lies with one of a number of charismatic, high profile investigator-writers, all of whom appear to encourage "their" witnesses to meet, talk, and provide support and confirmation for each others' experiences. It would almost be possible to see them in a "priest and confessor" role, if we wanted to take the comparison that far. Or to find close parallels with the charismatic leaders of millennial groups in the Middle Ages.

Having made the link with religions and belief groups, it's only a short step to link the life-changing interventions believed in by abductees with the life-changing interventions believed in by many of the groups and individuals we've considered in this book. For me, they are very much the same, and I suspect that both the underlying experiences, and the way people handle them, have distinct similarities. My own, personal view is that there is no objective, physical, dependable proof for any account of abduction by aliens, and that the promises that we would be given evidence in the form of implants, injuries, missing fœtuses and the rest have never been fulfilled. But the experiences appear to seem real enough to many of those who report them, however the memories are recovered or obtained. The way that abductees share their experiences, act on what they've learned in them and tell them to the world, the way their lives become filled with their missions, and the reverence they show for their leaders place the abduction experience firmly in a much older tradition. All are communicating, interacting, directly with their gods. All are conforming to a similar urge to believe in contact and intervention as the end of the century approaches.

Chapter 15

THE MODERN PROPHETS AND
THE NEXT TEN YEARS

You'll have realised by now that most millennial prophecy doesn't expect everything to happen in a day or two. The Christian versions usually involve a cycle of seven years of horror on Earth, New Age ones a few years as the process of Ascension takes place. The hybrids and abductions people know that those spaceships are filling up with strange grey crossbred children, but they can't say quite when we become inhabitants of the cosmos. The pole shift, earthquake, conjunction and comet brigade – and watch out for Comet Hale-Bopp, just starting to appear in prophecies of doom as I write – do expect immediate disaster, but most expect some of us to live on to thrive, eventually, in a finer and purer world.

So yes, there are the predictions that tell us what will happen down to the very day, or month, but there are plenty that don't. All are probably equally important. There are plenty of older prophecies that point directly or indirectly to the end of this century, and we've looked at many of them.

There are also many modern prophets, from all kinds of backgrounds. They prophesy different versions of dramatic endings and new beginnings, and new details are emerging all the time. In this last set of prophecies I've brought together some representatives of this breed of modern prophets, from the most Fundamentalist Christian to the most exotic New Age. If these people met each other I doubt that they'd want to discuss their predictions. Actually, they'd probably come to blows, or accuse each other of being possessed by demons, or being government agents working towards the New World Order. That's what they do in writing. They all see themselves as doing something radically different, but observed from outside, it looks like they could all be receiving their inspiration from very similar sources.

Jeanine Sautron and Roy Lemke –
Seventh-day Adventists, the Remnants

Of all the organisations and individuals who have sent me information to help write this book, much the most generous have been the Christian followers of evangelist Roy Lemke, who publishes the dreams and visions of living prophetess Jeanine Sautron as part of the work of the Dreams and Visions Evangelistic Center in Oregon. Highly organised, and familiar with modern communications, they have spent a substantial amount of money on sending me parcels of well-designed and original material, books, flyers, cassettes and computer disks, together with a civilised personal letter. This is a very different approach to others I have contacted, and to that of some New Age organisations in particular.

Jeanine Sautron's prophecies, translated from the French, are copious, and are often written in similar terms to the Book of Revelation. Dealing with specific events in relation to an imminent end of the world, they apparently come directly from Jesus, and are firmly based in the Bible. In 1993 she was writing of the beginnings of dramatic changes from 1995 onwards, and of a 12-year period of suffering which would be "shortened" by a merciful God.

The Remnants are opposed to other versions of the Seventh-day Adventists, and describe themselves as "conservative Christians who do not own guns, and do not believe in killing under any circumstance", a relief after the aggression of many fundamentalist groups. They also practice strict abstinence from sexuality, and vegetarianism, because the body is the Temple of the Holy Spirit. I am not aware of the extent of the Remnants' membership.

In his letter to me, Roy Lemke explained that: "We are intensely interested in the soon return of Jesus Christ in the clouds of glory, and we are looking forward to that great event with great anticipation. Our focus, as you may already know, though, is to give the full warning message of Revelation 14, warning the world not to receive 'the mark of the beast', the 'name' of the beast, or the 'number of his name', '666'; to come out of Babylon (the fallen churches)." He also explains the appreciation of the Remnants around the world for "the wonderful work of Margaret Thatcher in holding back the institution of the 'mark of the beast'."

The Remnants also hold in high esteem the End Times prophecies – apparently relating to the 1990s – made by Ellen White in an 1884 book called *The Great Controversy*. Their expectation is that all the plagues and horrors of Revelation will happen to us over the next nine years or so, and that the USA will be responsible for the imposition of the Mark of the Beast. They expect nuclear war, and a physical battle of

Armageddon. Yet they retain a great faith in the salvation of all believers, and their commitment, the task that they have taken on as a group, is to ensure that there are as many believers as possible, not cursed by accepting the dreaded Mark. If you're interested in real-life modern prophets, and specific prophecies, the Remnants would be worth your time and attention.

Stan Deyo

Editor of *WATT's News*, published from Perth, Western Australia, Stan Deyo is part prophet, part futurist, part reporter of all sorts of predictions. He has well-established interests in Atlantis, Free Energy, Anti-Gravity devices, the Biblical End Times Scenario, and various conspiracy theories and cover-ups.

His latest speciality is looking for earthquakes – before they happen, not after. He does this by accessing a US Navy web site on the Internet, which shows sea surface temperature maps. He compares these over several days, and says that it is apparent where temperatures are increasing surprisingly rapidly, suggesting that earthquake activity is beginning. In order to rule out the effects of storm activity he accesses further information supplied by the US Navy's FNMOC (Fleet Numerical Meteorology and Oceanography Center) which shows wave heights. He then predicts the time and place of earthquakes, sometimes successfully.

To this fairly scientific enterprise, Deyo adds a broad commitment to the Christian concept of the end of the world, and looks for evidence of changes in weather, health and social behaviour which suggest that end is near. What he finds on the Internet suggests that it is going to be one of the least reliable sources for writers and researchers: I'm wondering whether every crackpot in the Western world is now on the net, churning out the product of their frustrations, desires, and overwhelming paranoia.

You can make what you wish of his dreams that suggest that because of a pole shift, Australia will soon be where Antarctica is now, covered with ice, but I don't know of anyone apart from Deyo who is bringing together so many different elements of the Millennium Consensus. In *WATT's News* you can find Fundamentalist Grant Jeffrey's "computers-cashless society-666, Mark of the Beast" theories, a blood-sucking beast in Puerto Rico, wave heights in the North Atlantic, meteors and the

Apocalypse, Nostradamus and more. And if I lived in Australia, and suspected that an earthquake might trigger a pole shift, and a pole shift
might cover my home in ice, I'd be looking out for earthquakes, too.

Hal Lindsey

Jokes about making profits would be quite out of order in this book,
but there certainly can be money in prophecy. If you added up all the
books that use the wonderfully out-of-copyright Nostradamus, you'd
come up with a very impressive number, but the prophetic author who
has achieved the highest sales of books under his own name has got to
be the American, Hal Lindsey. His two greatest sellers were *The Late
Great Planet Earth* and *Satan is Alive and Well on Planet Earth*. They
were first published in 1970 and 1972, and have sold in their millions.

Lindsey – who wrote with the assistance of a professional freelance
author – was a former Mississippi river boat captain who attended the-
ological school and then worked for the Campus Crusade for Christ, a
very effective organisation that evangelised hard among students across
America. He certainly learned his trade well.

His work combined the standard elements of Daniel, Revelation and
other threatening parts of the Bible with a hefty dose of the "signs of
the times". In *Late Great Planet Earth* he traded on the fears and illu-
sions of right-wing America in a time when the political movements of
the young had found a common cause in the horrors of Vietnam, the
Cold War was at its coldest, and the threat of the Chinese and the
Soviets could be made to seem immediate and final. Lindsey would
find a few verses of scripture, then link it with his view of world events.
In a chapter sensitively titled "The Yellow Peril", he explains that the
Greek words translated as "east" in Revelation 16:12 were actually ana-
toles heliou, "the rising of the sun." This, says Lindsey, "was the ancient
designation of the Oriental races and nations. John describes this vast
horde of soldiers assembled at the Euphrates River as "the kings of the
sun rising" and thus definitely predicts the movement of a vast Oriental
army into a war in the Middle East."

There is much of the same. To explain Ezekiel's reference to cavalry
being used in the End Times invasion of Israel, he mentions that the
Cossacks have always loved horses, and that the Red Chinese used
them during the Korean War. He is convinced of a dramatic alliance
between Black Africa and the Soviet Union in the invasion of Israel that

will fulfil Daniel 11:36-45, and states that Africa "will become converted to Communism". Much prophecy depended on the continued existence of a Communist Soviet Union; the break-up of the Soviet Union
has been a great disappointment to many believers.

While *Late Great* doesn't actually indulge itself in dates, the contemporary reader was left with little doubt that the end of the world
was imminent – by the end of the eighties, at any rate. *Satan is Alive
and Well on Planet Earth* followed a similar line, but cashing in on the
popularity of *The Exorcist*, and the undeniable rise of interest in esoteric, occult and paranormal subjects. It traced the rise of Satan in the
world as a "sign of the times", to match the social and political elements
set out in *Late Great*. The overall message was the same – the end is
coming soon, and it's time you became a Christian because the alter-
natives don't bear thinking about!

In 1994, Lindsey published *Planet Earth 2000 AD*, which adapts
some of his earlier prophecies to the unexpected facts. Russia no
longer converts Black Africa to Communism, and instead becomes
involved in an alliance with the forces of Islam, and is more or less
dragged into a joint invasion of Israel. Before that, the Russians have
invaded Egypt, only turning their attentions to Israel when they hear
that the European forces are about to invade, and the Chinese are on
the move. The Europeans bomb the Russians, and the Euphrates River
has dried up so the 200 million Chinese can attack the Europeans at
Megiddo. Yes, it's the Battle of Armageddon that Lindsey knows must
take place before the Second Coming for which he's still anxiously waiting. We can watch out for his scenarios coming true – he's definitely a
part of the Millennium Consensus, even though it may be his second
try.

Stelle, Illinois

As long ago as 1979, the people of Stelle, Illinois predicted that civilisation will be destroyed by violent volcanic eruptions in May of 2000 AD.
They had chosen to live together in this new village, and prepare for the
future, because they believed that the great conjunction of planets of 5
May 2000 would do this final damage. In common with some of the Great
Pyramid interpreters, and the Jehovah's witnesses, they were convinced
that Armageddon had begun in 1914, but they also foresaw a dreadful
last war which would begin in 1998, and end in November 1999.

They were reported to be "working like beavers to build a fleet of lighter-than-air vehicles capable of floating above this terrestrial tumult". The plan was apparently to take the people of Stelle to a "city in the Pacific". They also wanted "to make a safe place for higher beings to incarnate in our community and join us in the Pacific. And we want to create the technology that will allow us to survive." They were said to be building, "an experimental energy-free home and a giant glasshouse for use after Armageddon".

Michael K Callagher – Christmas Day, 1999

From New Zealand, New Jerusalem Publications produced two booklets, one – *Gog, the Forces of Magog, The Land of America* – interpreting Ezekiel 38 and the visions of Daniel, and the other – *Christmas, the Two Witnesses and the Resurrection Connection* – the Book of Revelation. Both have clear prophecies for the Millennium, and were sent to me in 1993 by their author, Michael K Callagher.

While he did predict that George Bush would lose the US election in 1992 – you might remember how Nostradamus, or someone on his behalf, got that one wrong – he also said that Clinton would be "assassinated, or killed in an accident – within a year". Over the ensuing years, he predicted, President Al Gore would lead the United Nations forces in defeating Iran. It seems that the Great Beast is a massive computer system, but that Al Gore is the brains and power behind it, and may well be the Antichrist. Anyway, come 25 December 1999:

"The American forces will invade Israel's disputed territory according to their United Nations Resolutions. Israel will retaliate with Nuclear missiles against the invading American forces, who shall be completely destroyed on the mountains of Israel. Also Europe united shall destroy the land of America with Nuclear missiles.

"On this same Christmas day a great miracle shall happen when many living people shall disappear off the face of the Earth.

The predicted events to happen on this particular Christmas day shall start the time-clock of seven more years to the end of society as we know it. When the new millennium shall bring the renewal of the ages."

An unusual reading of events, this: the Rapture and the invasion of Israel on the same day, 25 December 1999. The invasion made by UN forces – not the Russians or Chinese – and an American Beast and Antichrist. You don't come across a lot of prophets from New Zealand!

Dannion Brinkley – Prophecy Near Death

Prophecies of events first published after they happened don't usually inspire much confidence. I worked briefly at a psychiatric hospital some years ago, where there was usually a television on to give the older and less mobile patients something to watch. Whenever a tragedy or disaster came on screen – an earthquake, a flood, an air crash, even a factory chimney falling on someone – one old lady would say, "I knew that would happen. I saw it in a dream weeks ago. I wish I could have warned them." And so on. It's a quick and easy way to make yourself feel bad for not doing something you probably couldn't do anyway. I understand this is not an uncommon phenomenon.

Dannion Brinkley published a very detailed and complex set of prophecies more than 15 years after he apparently became aware of them. This isn't to suggest that he wasn't aware of these prophecies before the events in them occurred, but when he published his hugely successful book *Saved by the Light*, even his publishers pointed out that "of the 117 revelations that he recalls, 95 have already come to pass." He also works with *Life After Life* author Dr Raymond Moody, one of the great advocates of the near-death experience. Brinkley claims, unusually, that he received the knowledge of his "revelations" during a near-death experience, some years before the concept of NDEs became popular.

Here, however, we should look at the prophecies, rather than their background. One really accurate, future prophecy could set aside any doubts I might have, so what of the 22 revelations that have not yet come to pass?

Brinkley's description of his experience reminds me of the original Book of Revelation. He travelled in a spiritual world, and arrived at a place where thirteen Beings of Light sat in a "magnificent lecture hall". He describes their emotions and characteristics, and then the revelations begin, in a modern version of the Patmos visions.

"The Beings came at me one at a time. As each one approached, a box the size of a videotape came from its chest and zoomed right at my face... but a moment before impact, the box opened to reveal what appeared to be a tiny television picture of a world event that was yet to happen... I felt myself drawn right into the picture, where I was able to live the event."

Brinkley's overall message is one of the USA's moral and spiritual decline, and this underpins the visions he saw. When he wrote the book – I think in 1993 – his so far unfulfilled prophecies included:

A Chernobyl-style nuclear accident, leading to "cancer victims and mutated babies in Russia, Norway, Sweden, and Finland, not hundreds or thousands of people, but tens of thousands, in a vast array of deformity... The date on the picture was 1995."

In a vision of "The Environmental Religion", reminiscent of both the Antichrist, and the Four Horsemen – "I saw the speaker from Russia as he talked with zeal about our need to heal the environment. People rallied round him quickly, and he soon became so powerful that he was elected one of the leaders of the United Nations. I saw this Russian riding on a white horse, and I knew that his rise would come before the year 2000".

A Sino-Soviet conflict, beginning with a battle over a railway, followed by the Chinese "cutting the country in half and taking over the oil fields of Siberia". These events follow "the death of Soviet Communism."

"A world in horrible turmoil by the turn of the century", with economic disaster that "would lead to the bankruptcy of America by the year 2000." There would also be two horrendous earthquakes in America "sometime before the end of the century".

Brinkley apparently foresaw the Desert Storm operation, and Egypt being taken over by religious fanatics by 1997. Before 2000, there will be "a chemical attack by Arabs on a city in France. A chemical is put into the water supply, and thousands drink it and die before it can be eliminated."

He saw visions of misery and destruction, including cannibalism around the world, and the 12th Being of Light showed him a computer chip being forcibly inserted under the skin of everyone in the world to control and, if desired, kill them. In a close parallel to the Great Beast and 666 scenarios, those who "refused to have chips implanted in their bodies roamed as outcasts. They could not be employed and were denied government services."

Although a Being of Light told him that these events might be avoided if humanity changed – a message frequently heard from the Virgin Mary – these are clear prophecies and predictions, and it will be possible to measure their success or failure. I anticipate that we will hear more of Dannion Brinkley and his range of extraordinary experiences.

David Hathaway – Prophetic Vision in Russia

David Hathaway is a British evangelist who has committed his efforts to converting the people of the former Soviet Union. Under the old regime he was jailed for smuggling Bibles, and his "Eurovision – Mission to Europe" publicity material claims that:

"In 1986 God showed David Hathaway that the Iron Curtain would collapse and, along with it, Communism. Revival would sweep from east to west – but then another curtain would come down... That curtain is beginning to fall across Russia today! Whatever the cost – spiritually, physically, financially – we must win Russia for Christ before it is too late."

Hathaway relies heavily on the standard Biblical sources for the underlying pattern of the future he foresees, but ties in real and specific worldly events about which he seems to have specialist knowledge. He also has frequent contact with God, as in a vision he had while preaching in February 1993:

"The challenge is that God is about to do the greatest miracles the world has ever seen. He's going to raise up prophets, He's going to raise up men like Elijah... There's going to be an enormous battle taking place in Europe and Russia. Satan is going to be defeated, his power is going to be broken!... We're living in the last days, the days of the return of Christ, the days when we are going to see the Revival Fire bursting on the Church... Those days are going to culminate with the sound of a trumpet, and that sound is going to echo from every building, until suddenly, in a blaze of Glory sweeping across the sky from the East to the West. Christ is going to come back to the Earth and take control!"

On 1 October 1995, during Hathaway's Ukraine crusade of 21 major meetings in little over two months, a "sign appeared in the sky above the Eurovision Crusade in Evpatoria. An open door in heaven, it remained over the ministry for three hours." Reproductions of photos of this sign are not very clear, but appear to show a brilliantly white light emitting from, or overlaying, a geometric shape or structure. The photo reproduced in Eurovision's campaign literature seems to be a Polaroid, so presumably there isn't a negative to be examined.

In the third issue of the magazine *Prophetic Vision*, Spring/Summer 1996, Hathaway examines the prospects for the next three or four years, and suggests that the Antichrist, "may well be revealed in Russia".

He mentions, as an aside, the Roman Catholic belief that 1999 will see "the Immaculate Heart of Mary" triumphing as a result of her intervention in Russia, and the *Weekly World News* story that in August 1995 President Bill Clinton met the last surviving descendant of Nostradamus, who "shared visions of the Russians re-establishing the Soviet Union by military force and launching an attack on Israel in 1999".

Hathaway's most specific speculation relates to the possible identity of the Antichrist. Quoting the Gog of Magog prophecies from Ezekiel 38 and 39, where a massive army attacks Israel from the north as part of the "End Times scenario". He says that "It would appear there is one man alive today who could fit and fulfil this prophecy: Vladimir Volfovitch Zhirinovsky," and points out that "Josephus, amongst other ancient historians, identifies Magog as Khazakstan – where Vladimir Zhirinovsky was born on 25 April 1946. Zhirinovsky is running for Russian President in the 1996 elections."

Giving us something specific to look out for – something that really could fit in with biblical prophecy – Zhirinovsky's book, *Last Dash to the South* apparently says:

"Our army will perform this task... The last dash to the south and Russia's outlet to the shores of the Indian Ocean and the Mediterranean Sea are really the task of saving the Russian nation... This is not just my whim. It is Russia's destiny. It is fate."

Hathaway asks: "Is it fate, or is it the fulfilment of the prophetic word of the Lord spoken through Ezekiel?" I look forward to receiving David Hathaway's updates. His must be a remarkable way of life.

Celestine Prophecies – the edges of reality

Can you imagine what sort of book of New Age discovery might be written by a middle-aged, North American white male, with a BA in Sociology, an MEd in Counselling, and 15 years' experience as a therapist? If you can, you may just have imagined something very like James Redfield's *The Celestine Prophecy*.

That is, if you haven't actually read it. This is a remarkable bestseller, which was quickly followed by *The Celestine Prophecy: An Experiential Guide*. A sequel, called *The Tenth Insight* has just been published. *The Celestine Prophecy* isn't, and this is important to note, a real prophecy. The book is a book of fiction, and stilted fiction at that. But it wouldn't be difficult to interpret the book as suggesting that the prophecies contained in are real, and the account of the circumstances of their discovery as true. The influence it has had on individuals, groups, and the New Age movement as a whole is so great that we should consider it in our investigation. Actually, the book offers the intelligent and informed reader insights that the author probably never intended. Insights into the sort of people who take books like this too seriously.

The plot wouldn't disgrace an Enid Blyton adventure. It's a sort of "Five go to Peru and discover nine ancient manuscripts in spite of the efforts of the Army and the Roman Catholic Church". I understand that the Peru in the book is a less than accurate one, and in the age of faxes, scanners, and ubiquitous photocopiers, the fear that the contents of a particular document will be lost forever if it is confiscated by the baddies – an essential and repeating element of the plot – is unconvincing.

However, Redfield has that *X-Files* touch, not only making events that have never happened and never will seem possible, but blaming our ignorance of their occurrence on "official", probably "government" interference. And the content of his "ancient manuscript" clearly has great appeal, although not to me.

The ancient manuscript in *The Celestine Prophecy* contains nine "Insights", which were supposedly written by a non-Christian priest very many years ago, and were apparently found in a ruined Inca city. These are summarised neatly in *The Experiential Guide*, which is sold as "The Essential Guide to Your Own Personal Adventure", and develop sequentially, from one through nine. They take the reader from a beginning of restlessness, "led forward by mysterious coincidences", and wanting to see spiritual development in their lives (First). This restlessness changes (Second) to an awareness of a "new, more complete worldview", understanding the purposes of humanity and the universe. This general awareness then develops in specific directions. The ability to "see" energy and the way it flows around and between humans and other living creatures (Three), and then (Four) understanding the "struggle for power" in controlling and containing that energy and its flow.

The Fifth Insight is called "The Message of the Mystics", and deals with the thrill of connection with the divine, and identifying when that connection is real. The Sixth presents the apparent need to analyse, understand and "clear" the past, in a very psycho-analytic manner. I am uncomfortable with this one.

The Seventh gets paranormal, as the coincidences build and involve other people in "synchronistically" providing wisdom and meeting needs. The Eighth again causes me trouble, limiting personal commitment to other individuals, limiting romance, almost limiting the numbers of children in the family, in order to pay full attention to the purposes of the Insights themselves.

The Ninth Insight – the last in the first book – sees our means of survival automated as we concentrate on our spiritual growth, moving into higher energy states, eventually leaving physical form behind, and defeating and avoiding life and death. New Age and Christian aspirations rolled into one.

So why is this called a prophecy, rather than the credo of an imaginary, or hoped-for cult? Simply, because it is presented to people who would like it to be true, as if it is true. That's both the people in the book, and the people who read it. If you're restless, if you look for coincidences and synchronicities, and you'd like to be connected to the divine, this is exactly the sort of book you're likely to buy. If you want to believe in the recollection of past lives, birth memories, and the recovery from what probably isn't your memory of other events which are pretty much resistant to the demands of evidence, I expect you'll enjoy *The Tenth Insight* as well.

If your life needs this kind of input, *The Celestine Prophecy* will provide you with more or less what you want: a clearly defined way to live, a belief in your own powers, and your place in a co-created Ascension of humanity. All that, and you can also identify with the characters' struggle against the forces of authority and repression, and rejoice in their success. As prophecies go, fictional as it is in the telling, it is likely to be as influential as any other that you'll find in this book.

Gordon-Michael Scallion

The solution to the crop circle mystery is just a small part of what self-styled futurist Gordon-Michael Scallion has to offer us. He publishes the *Earth Changes Report*, a glossy monthly, and appeals equally to the survivalist, the new age, and the lost knowledge groups in a market offering great opportunities for messages of this kind.

Crop circles are, it seems, made by "The Ethereans", who live in the "fifth Earth Realm", and are in contact with "those who were a portion of the earlier root races on Earth – Pleiades and Sirius". The Ethereans and the Pleiadeans together make the crop circles.

Scallion also has a wealth of information about the world's past. Light-beings first arrived here some 18 million years ago, and not till 1.5 million years ago did life-forms become sufficiently "physical in vibration" to "be understood today". The continent of Pan was destroyed in a pole-shift, their civilisation to be followed by that of Atlan and then, about 70,000 years ago by the "golden age of Lemuria". Further revelations about our history are promised.

But it is difficult to verify claims of this kind. Actually, it's completely impossible: writing unwritten history is a remarkably safe bet. Scallion, however, is as happy predicting the future as explaining the past. As a prophet, he is unusually specific, daring even.

His lines of communication with other intelligences seem to be a mixture of a form of automatic writing on to a computer, when he enters "a timestream", together with more traditional visionary experiences. I am not sure whether he sees himself as particularly chosen for these communications, or why he has these abilities.

Scallion does not see an absolute end of the world by the year 2000, but links dramatic spiritual changes with horrifying physical ones. He publishes a four-colour "Future Map of the United States: 1998-2001" which shows "how and where California will fracture and become known as the Isles of California: how Phoenix will become a seaport: where the new West Coast will be: how the Mississippi River will become an inland seaway", and a video, *Tribulation: The Coming Earth Changes*, which provides information about other parts of the world as well. There will be a great many deaths and a lot of suffering if these predictions are right.

Like most successful prophets, Scallion offers a form of salvation or escape. In physical terms, this is advice on "safe areas". Where those who buy his publications can go to escape the changes he foresees. However, appealing as being a survivor may be, there is always a chance that you're wasting your time. He predicted that Mount Rainier, a volcano in Washington State, would erupt as earthquakes hit Washington and Oregon. Writing in the August 1994 issue of *ECR*, he said that Seattle would be severely damaged by the explosion of an eruption on the southwest side of Rainier, and by associated earthquakes, and ash.

The West Coast of the USA from Vancouver to Mexico would shake, and the islands in Puget Sound would experience tidal waves and quakes. This would all happen, "Between 1993 through 1995". I'm no expert on North American seismology, and I know that earthquakes of one kind or another are occurring all the time. But I don't recall Seattle meeting its predicted fate.

Other specific predictions include the US, post-disaster, being organised into 13 Colonies. There is to be a nuclear accident, similar to Chernobyl, to the east of the Rockies, which will result from dilapidated equipment, not from the earth changes. This will lead to the revival of the anti-nuclear movement, and eventually to the safer and more useful disposal of spent fuel.

He also predicts a Third World War, beginning between 1995 and 1998, which does little harm to the USA. Turkey will be the first country to suffer a nuclear attack, followed by nine unnamed others. Interestingly, he describes this conflict as occurring in, "The time of the AntiChrist's reign of terror – or right after nuclear war begins in Africa and the Middle East." Biblical references find their way into most prophetic material, even when it has no apparent Christian or Jewish basis. Responsibility for the nuclear attacks will apparently be claimed by a group claiming to be acting on God's behalf.

The spiritual elements of the predicted Earth Changes are fairly standard new age ones, with thought creating reality, and making life better and richer. After, presumably, we have finished burying our children, and when we aren't engaged in trying to ensure the post-nuclear survival of much of the world's population.

Chapter 16

THE LAST ROUND-UP?

So how do you write the conclusion to a book about the end of the world? Well, with great care for a start. If I've learned one sad truth in 28 years of working with and writing about extraordinary beliefs, it's that it is very easy to make people afraid, and very difficult to put fear out of their minds. So far, the best antidote I've found to fear is knowledge, and the understanding that comes from knowledge. Providing some of that knowledge has been the primary motivation in writing this book. I hope my plan has worked.

I recognise that it won't have worked for everyone. There will be those who become fearful because of what they have read here, probably because they've picked out bits and pieces that interested them, and haven't balanced one set of prophecies or predictions with another, or considered the failures along with the successes. If you're one of those people, this conclusion is particularly for you.

I was recently asked by a radio station to record an interview for a phone-in they were going to run about end-times prophecies. I asked them what title they were running it under, and was told "Fear of the Millennium". I politely declined their offer, because I've learned how these things go. The discussion in programmes of that kind is usually set up by a long list of doom and gloom prophecies, and only then does the discussion begin. Even then, phone-ins – and I've guested on a few in the past – attract callers who want to impress others with their views, however daft or unpleasant those views might be. They can sell whatever craziness they choose without being made to explain or defend it. How much more fear do we all need?

A Matter of Time

I can give you good reasons for believing that the prophecies we've considered in this book shouldn't make us any more concerned about our future than it is natural and wise to be.

Firstly, there's the question of time, and the way that I understand time works. I know that there are fans of the new physics out there who'll tell me I'm wrong, but I support the view that time is pretty much a straight line. With occasional exceptions, we can only go forwards along it as time passes and takes us with it, and we can only go backwards through the memories of ourselves and others. There may be incidents which avoid that general rule, like premonitions of individual death and disaster, which seem to be based in some way on a foreknowledge of deeply emotional, heart-rending experiences. Personal bereavement leads to crisis apparitions that occur on or around the moment of death, as the dying mind seems to reach out to someone it loves and needs. Impersonal premonitions may relate to the way in which media reports affect individuals. A vague understanding of what is to happen occasionally comes to a few individuals, in a dream or a vision that might derive from newspaper or television coverage that will only appear after the event takes place. The detail of these premonitions is seldom good enough to identify the event before it occurs.

While it's hard to understand those little slips in time, and I don't pretend to know how they come about, what our prophets promise us is usually on a completely different scale. What sense can we make of the threats and promises made by the religious visions? The Rapture, Antichrist, Great Beast, Armageddon, Second Coming, Last Judgment sequence is said to be inevitable, ordained by God from at least the time of the visions that led to the books of Daniel and Revelation. The only question to ask about it is "when?", not "if". But how is that meant to fit with the messages given by the more recent, more personal visions, particularly those involving the Virgin Mary. If time runs on that line, surely the hideous end promised to an immoral world will either happen or not. How could it be that it can be threatened, again and again, and then withdrawn, again and again. It's hard to believe in a future that's conditional on the personal conduct of small groups of believers all over the world, who often know nothing of the messages given to the others.

And talking of time again, who is it that provides the information to prophets like Nostradamus, or the person who pretended to be St Malachy, or to Gordon-Michael Scallion, or Dannion Brinkley? Are we in a sort of "Akashic Records" situation, where all the events of the past, present and future are lodged in a gigantic library somewhere, if only we could just get access to them? Are these people granted that access, or is there an intermediary who teases humanity with bits and pieces of information, most of it wrong, and just the occasional fragment right? Whenever you hear that someone is predicting the future, ask yourself how they know, who's told them, where on earth information like that has come from. And if somebody out there, or up there, or down there really does know what's going to happen, because it's all fixed and immovable, then how much does it matter what we think, or do? What choices do we have?

Which brings us to the second good reason for not worrying about the prophecies about our future. Simply, they can't all be true because they are so different. They just can't all happen. Not even most of them can happen. The Second Coming of Christ and the Last Judgment don't begin to fit with the New Age. The aliens of the channellers have nothing in common with the aliens abducting people across the USA. The world can't end in 1999, and in 2006, and in 2012, any more than it did in all the dates predicted in the past. The Great Tribulation can't last both three days and seven years. We can't be both in Heaven, and on top of a mountain waiting for rescue by UFOs. We can't be both in Hell, and drowning in the flood as California is covered by the sea.

These contradictions will lead many people to make a choice, and stick with it. They'll pick one prophecy and one prophet, and wait and believe till that prophecy comes true. Or it doesn't. Personally, I'm yet to be that impressed with any one prophecy that I'd put my faith in it. I'm choosing to apply the lessons I've learned in writing this book, that in all the history of prediction and anticipation, very little comes true. And what does is mostly on a personal and private scale.

Watching and Waiting

I like to think that I'll spend the next few years doing what Charles Fort, for whom *Fortean Times* is named, might have done himself if he had the opportunity to see in the Millennium. I'm going to watch very closely what's going on, report it in my Millennium Watch in *Fortean Times*, and wait and see how the current crop of prophecies turn out. And what new ones come along.

Which should keep me reasonably busy. In the past two weeks, I've received details of predictions sent from a variety of high-powered galactic intelligences like Ashtar and Sananda. All agree that the landing of 15 million flying saucers, recognising mankind's spiritual breakthrough and ascension to a higher plane of spiritual existence, will begin in September 1996. At least two more predictions of the identity of the Antichrist emerged from the final week of the elections for the Russian Presidency. There are, it seems, three more recent appearances of the Virgin Mary ongoing, complete with messages and associated healings, which I need to know more about. No doubt at least one will involve prophecy and warnings. One of the quality UFO magazines arrived from the USA a few days ago, offering new understandings of the purpose of the alien abductors, and how we should interpret their intentions for our future. The Millennium Consensus keeps on developing in extraordinary directions.

Looking for the Signs

This will be a fascinating and exciting few years. We'll run through the prophecies we know have been made for these times, the prophecies we can watch come true, or be proved as wrong as so many others. But first, let's think about what we can look out for ourselves, what sorts of signs make the prophets do what they do.

The key signs will be seen in the way our society deteriorates. Actually, I don't necessarily think that it will deteriorate that much, or that badly, but every generation sees decay and degeneration in the next, and with the kind of "moral majority" politics prevalent on both sides of the Atlantic it will be easy to interpret inevitable change as divinely-ordained tribulation. The fundamentalist Christians who concluded that AIDS was a plague sent by an angry God to clear the homosexuals out of his creation typify this kind of thinking. If that was God's intention, then He's made a rotten and inaccurate job of it.

Weather and natural events will be important. Environmental and green issues play a major role in much New Age thinking, and one kind of risk gets confused with another. Predictions and fears of earthquakes, of pole shifts, of melting ice, of glaciation, all appear regularly in the literature of the Millennium. We will certainly hear a lot more of comets and asteroids that might, but probably won't, come somewhere near the Earth. The ancient terrors of natural phenomena persist unabated, and eclipses and conjunctions of planets will play their part in the growth of millennial belief, despite the ability of our science to predict and understand them. No doubt there will be many more messages and visitations, and more of those charismatic individuals who always emerge out of countries in crisis, concerned more with leadership than with truth, and care, and honesty. There are plenty of lessons to be had, and we will do well to be wary of following anyone who looks to enlist us to publicise their beliefs, or offers to take us with them wherever they say they're going.

The Controllers

It's clear that we shouldn't lump all the prophets and interpreters together, and say that they have the same personality defects, the same weaknesses, that they are all mad or bad. That's the sort of approach adopted by the mindless skeptics, the debunkers who look no further than how the beliefs of others compare to their own. "You're wrong, I'm different from you, so I must be right" has always been a very poor argument, but it's used all too often. Consider the treatment handed out to William Miller and the Millerites, how good and genuine intentions, based on years of careful study and calculation, have become characterised as arrogant and stupid. The same rich, big-name evangelists who criticise people like Miller seem to calculate their control over their own followers with a prevailing interest in commercial success, keeping those dollars rolling in. I know who I consider more honourable. Honourable, too, were the Native American end times beliefs and others like them, as cultures struggled to survive against the arrogance of outsiders.

Of course, there are some very unpleasant people around, and end times scenarios, carefully presented, offer them unique opportunities to control and exploit others. I hope we'll all watch out for the charismatic figures who are certain to emerge in the next few years, making predictions, and promising salvation. The tradition of threat and promise is an ancient one in many faiths and beliefs, but it doesn't only emerge in traditional religious movements. It's also been adopted by countless others. Think of Bo and Peep, of David Koresh and Waco, the White Brotherhood, Aum Supreme Truth, and the Order of the Solar Temple. All of these groups were built round individuals who, whatever their personal beliefs, delighted in controlling and exploiting others, and found the perfect way of doing it. Where I can, I'll try and challenge people like these in future: I hope some of you out there might join me if the chance arises.

The Great Beast and the Antichrist

At least three of the candidates in the elections for the Russian Presidency were accused of being the Antichrist, or the Great Beast. It was particularly odd seeing that some of these accusations had been made by the Communist contender – I didn't think he believed in that kind of thing. We know that the Emperor Nero was a prime target, and more recently Napoleon and Hitler have been obvious targets. In the last decade the finger has been pointed at Bill Clinton – because of his supposed New World Order links – and at Al Gore, mainly because of his very public interest in computers. The Reverend Ian Paisley has publicly, and in person, called the Pope the Antichrist. It's a not uncommon concept in extreme Protestant circles, but then the extreme right-wing Catholics have their own clear ideas about identity, too. Accusations and guesses like these will persist over the next few years.

Ones to watch

I could have included more prophecies in this book, but most of them would have been either New Age, channelled from an invisible denizen of the universe to some lonely soul, earthbound till the coming Ascension. Or they would have been based on yet more interpretations of Daniel and Revelation. I'm confident that I've covered examples of all the current kinds of prophecy – confident till I'm proved wrong, anyway!

So, what should we look out for over the next four or five years? If the next Pope can be identified by the words Gloriae Olivae, keep an eye on St Malachy, and the Pope after next. If one of the Garabandal visionaries gives the eight days' notice promised of The Warning, look out for photos of phenomena in the pine trees in the village. If Atlantis is really rediscovered, read the rest of the predictions of Edgar Cayce.

The dependability of the Great Pyramid as a source of prophecy increasingly depends on the discovery in 1999 of amazing subterranean buildings, full of the knowledge of the ancient world. Also in 1999, the Great King of the Mongols should be up and about again, as promised by Nostradamus. The knowledge of the Mayans probably won't be tested till 2012, but should the purported Hopi prophecies of nuclear war come about, we'll probably be beyond caring who was right or wrong. The same goes for the earth-shaking "flood and earthquake" prophecies of Gordon-Michael Scallion, and the encroaching ice-caps dreamed of by Stan Deyo and others.

If Jeanine Sautron and Roy Lemke have it right, we'll be well advised to choose not to accept the Mark of the Beast, but we'll have to make that choice in the next three years or so. If Hal Lindsey knows what he's talking about, the Chinese are going to be taking over a lot more than Hong Kong before the end of the decade. David Hathaway seems to be in broad agreement with him.

The predictions of Michael Callagher promise us a miserable Christmas in 1999, but few prophecies are quite as grim – or quite so inordinately well-publicised – as those of Dannion Brinkley, who promises worldwide cannibalism and far worse by the end of the century.

Fortunately – and Brinkley is a good example, because his "Beings of Light" are already proving to be less bright than they might have appeared – the chances are that little if any of this will really happen. The history of prophecy is one of people being persistently and thoroughly wrong, which means that their mysterious, other-worldly informants, or their books of scripture, or whatever else they used to arrive at their predictions were also, generally, completely mistaken. This shouldn't detract from the good intentions of many prophets, their belief that they are genuinely doing what is right. If I had a premonition that an airliner was going to crash, I'd try to warn people not to travel on it. If I thought there was going to be a tremendous flash-flood where I live, I'd take precautions to find high ground for my family before it hit, and I hope I'd persuade others to do the same.

It doesn't seem possible to explain why many thousands of people, over thousands of years, have become convinced that they know what the future holds. But they have, and they will, and we'll continue to be interested in what they have to say. These people will, I promise you, almost all be completely mistaken about the future. They always have been, and none of us should worry on account of what they predict.

Because some of these people will be driven by a desire to hurt, and control, and exploit, we should be wary, and willing to take issue with those individuals. Mostly, they will be harmless, and they'll often turn out to be people of genuine goodwill, who want to help the rest of us, and make the world a better place. I rather like these people, and their willingness to try to change what they think needs changing. I find it fascinating that there are more of them than ever, and that they broadly agree that those changes will occur, and when they will take place. I suspect that this Millennium Consensus, just by its very existence, may have some effect on our futures.

So far as external intervention is concerned, whether by Gods, or aliens, the Great White Brotherhood, the Holy Spirit, King Arthur, the Virgin Mary or anybody else, I am unconvinced. In working out what the future will be like I think that the choices, and the responsibilities, still remain ours, and ours alone.

Chapter 17

REFERENCES & BIBLIOGRAPHY

Some of the subjects in this book are ones I've been researching and writing about for years, and I can't give you references for all the information that's included here. Some of it I just happen to know, and some comes from my own written work and notes. However, I've delved into a lot of new and unfamiliar material, too, and I've found more material than I'd ever expected. In putting these references together, I've tried to give you enough information to pursue my research a bit further, or to check on my accuracy if you wish to do so.

As you may be aware, the worlds of prophecy and contact with non-human intelligence are reported as much in magazines, pamphlets and publicity material as they are in books. With a handful of dependable exceptions I haven't given details of magazines, though some are mentioned in the text. They come and go, and I don't want readers wasting money on magazines they might never receive. Consequently, I've just listed the other main, identifiable sources that I've used. If you need further information, want to point out any mistakes, or come across anything you think would be interesting if we go on to produce another edition, I'll be happy to hear from you through *Fortean Times*.

Apocalypse, Plague & Judgment

Several versions of the Bible.

Lorie, Peter. *Revelation*. London: Boxtree, 1995.

Morris, L. *The Tyndale New Testament Commentaries – Revelation*. Leicester: IVP 1987.

Phillips, JB. translated. *The Book of Revelation*. London: Geoffrey Bles, 1957.

Shaw, Eva. *Eve of Destruction – Prophecies, Theories and Preparations for the End of the World*. Chicago: Contemporary Books, 1995.

The Christian End Times

Greed, John A. *The Next Twenty Years – Is It Armageddon or Aquarius?* Bristol: St Trillo Publications, 1979.

Jeffrey, Grant A. *Final Warning – Economic Collapse and the Coming World Government*. Toronto: Frontier Research Publications, 1995.

Lightner, Robert P. *The Last Days Handbook – A Comprehensive Guide to Understanding the Different Views of Prophecy*. Nashville: Thomas Nelson, 1990.

Pawson, David. *Explaining the Second Coming*. Kent: Sovereign World, 1993.

Walvoord, John F. *The Rapture Question*. Grand Rapids: Zondervan Books, 1979.

Watson, Sydney. *The Mark of the Beast*. Bible Institute of Los Angeles, 1918.

Watson, Sydney. *In the Twinkling of an Eye*. London: W. Nicholson & Sons.

A History of Failure

Clark, Elmer T. *The Small Sects in America*. Nashville: Cokesbury Press, 1937.

Cohn, Norman. *The Pursuit of the Millennium – Revolutionary Millenarians and Mystical Anarchists of the Middle Ages*. London: Granada, 1970.

Eliade, Mircea (Editor in Chief). *Encyclopaedia of Religion*. New York: MacMillan & Free Press, 1987.

Gratus, Jack. *The False Messiahs*. London: Victor Gollancz, 1975.

Harrison, JFC. *The Second Coming – Popular Millenarianism 1780–1850*. London: Routledge & Kegan Paul, 1979.

Lanternari, Vittorio. *The Religions of the Oppressed – A Study of Modern Messianic Cults*. London: MacGibbon & Kee, 1963.

The Nostradamus Problem

Beckley, Timothy Green. *Nostradamus' Unpublished Prophecies*. New Jersey, Inner Light, 1991.

Brennan, J H. *Nostradamus – Visions of the Future.* Aquarian, 1992.

Cheetham, E. *The Prophecies of Nostradamus.* Corgi, 1973.

de Fontbrune, J-C. *Nostradamus 1: Countdown to Apocalypse.* Pan, 1983.

de Fontbrune, J-C. *Nostradamus 2: Into the Twenty-First Century.* Hutchinson, 1984.

Hewitt, VJ and Lorie, P. *The End of the Millennium – Prophecies: 1992 to 2001.* Simon & Schuster, 1991.

Lorie, P (Astrological Consultant Dr Liz Greene). *Nostradamus, The Millennium and Beyond – The Prophecies to 2016.* Bloomsbury, 1993.

Randi, J. *The Mask of Nostradamus – The Prophecies of the World's Most Famous Seer.* New York: Prometheus, 1993.

Robb, S. *Nostradamus on Napoleon, Hitler and the Present Crisis.* USA: Scribner's, 1941.

Robb, S. *Nostradamus – Prophecies on World Events.* New York: Liveright Publishing Corporation, 1961.

Roberts, Henry C. *The Complete Prophecies of Nostradamus.* Corgi, 1985.

Ward, Chas A. *Oracles of Nostradamus.* New York: Dorset Press, 1891/1986.

Woolf, HI. *Nostradamus – King of Prophets, Prophet of Kings.* Resurgam, 1944.

Messages from Mary

Brochado, Costa. *Fatima in the Light of History.* Milwaukee: The Bruce Publishing Company, 1955.

De la Sainte Trinite, Frere Michel. *The Whole Truth About Fatima – The Secret and the Church.* New York: Immaculate Heart Publications, 1989.

De Marchi, John. *Fatima the Facts.* Cork: Mercier Press, 1954.

Flynn, Ted and Maureen. *The Thunder of Justice.* USA: MaxKol Communications,1993.

Gouin, Abbe. *Sister Mary of the Cross – Shepherdess of La Salette.* Wolverhampton: Marian Centre for Unitas Catolica, 1981.

McClure, Kevin. *The Evidence for Visions of the Virgin Mary.* Wellingborough: Aquarian, 1983.

Sister Lucia. *Fatima in Lucia's Own Words.* Fatima: Postulation Centre, 1989.

Stanford, Ray. *Fatima Prophecy – a pscychic channels the controversial prophecy of Fatima for the New Age.* 1988.

The Future in the Past

Carter, Mary Ellen. *Edgar Cayce on Prophecy.* New York: Warner, 1972.

Collin de Plancy, J. *La Fin Des Temps – confirmee par des propheties authentiques.* Paris: Henri Plon, 1874.

Davidson, D and Aldersmith, H. *The Great Pyramid – Its Divine Message.* London: William & Norgate, 1948.

Edgar, Morton. *The Great Pyramid – Its Spiritual Symbolism.* Glasgow: Bone & Hulley, 1924.

Mann, AT. *Millennium Prophecies.* Shaftesbury: Element, 1992.

Robinson, Lytle W. *Is it true what they say about Edgar Cayce?* Jersey: Neville Spearman, 1975.

Windsor, Diana. *Mother Shipton's Prophecy Book.* Knaresborough: Mother Shipton's Cave Ltd, 1990.

There's Nothing Worse than a God Who Gets His Facts Wrong

Dixon, Jeane, (as told to Rene Noorbergen). *My Life and Prophecies.* London: Frederick Muller, 1969.

Evans, Hilary with Spencer, John (compiled and edited). *UFOs 1947–1987 – the 40-year search for an explanation*. East Ham: Fortean Tomes, 1987.

Festinger, L, Riecken, HW, and Schachter, S. *When Prophecy Fails – a social and psychological study of a modern group that predicted the destruction of the world*. New York: Harper Torchbooks, 1964.

Pate, C, Marvin, and Haines, Calvin B Jr. *Doomsday Delusions – What's Wrong with Predictions about the End of the World*. Illinois: IVP,.1995.

Armed and Dangerous
Linedecker, Clifford L. *Massacre at Waco*. London: True Crime, 1993.

Dissenters
Cohn, Norman. *Cosmos, Chaos and the World to Come – the ancient roots of apocalyptic faith*. New York and London: Yale University Press, 1993.

Ma'sumian, Farnaz. *Life After Death – a study of the afterlife in world religions*. Oxford: One World Publications, 1995.

The Beginning of the New Age
Ferguson, Marilyn. *The Aquarian Conspiracy – Personal and Social Transformation in the 1980s*. London: Granada, 1981.

Joslin, Linda J. *Advent Calendar for the Salvation of the Planet Earth*. Bath: Gateway, 1995.

The Bible and the New World Order
Icke, David. *The Robots' Rebellion – The Story of the Spiritual Renaissance*. Bath: Gateway, 1994.

Lobster magazine. As I write it costs £2.50 for a substantial issue from the editor, Robin Ramsay, 214 Westbourne Avenue, Hull, HU5 3JB, UK

The Blessing – Holy and Unholy Spirits
Hill, Clifford and others. *Blessing the Church? – the history and direction of the Charismatic Movement and the impact of the Toronto Blessing*. Surrey: Eagle, 1995.

Alpha and *Renewal* are magazines that report on events and beliefs in the charismatic and evangelical movements. Both can be found in Christian bookshops.

Hybrids and High Strangeness
Hopkins, Budd. *Missing Time*. New York: Ballantine, 1981.

Jacobs, David M. *Secret Life*. London: Fourth Estate, 1993.

Mack, John E. *Abduction – Human Encounters with Aliens*. London: Simon & Schuster, 1994.

Streiber, W. *Communion*. London: Century, 1987.

Magonia magazine covers the issues of alien abductions in depth. £1.50 an issue from John Rimmer, John Dee Cottage, 5 James Terrace, Mortlake Churchyard, London, SW14 8HB UK.

The Modern Prophets and the Next Ten Years
Brinkley, Dannion, with Perry, Paul. *Saved by the Light*. London: Piatkus, 1994.

Lindsey, Hal. *The Late Great Planet Earth*. London: Lakeland, 1970.

Lindsey, Hal. *Satan is Alive and Well on Planet Earth*. New York: Bantam, 1972.

Redfield, James. *The Celestine Prophecy – An Adventure*. London: Bantam, 1994.

Redfield, James and Adrienne, Carol. *The Celestine Prophecy – An Experiential Guide*. London: Bantam, 1995.

INDEX

The Fortean Times Book of Inept Crime

Compiled by Steve Moore

Even Inspector Clouseau could have caught the staggeringly inept criminals who…

- Hid the live lobsters they were stealing by stuffing them down their underpants – with agonising consequences
- Walked into a bank to warn staff they would be back in half an hour to hold them up
- Broke into an unmarked – but occupied –police car in their search for a getaway vehicle
  and
- Glued themselves securely to the floor while robbing a solvent factory

As well as covering inept crime in all its glory, this latest in the popular *Fortean Times Book of…* series also includes chapters on incongruous, bizarre, and apparently occult crimes: the man who escaped from a high security prison using only dental floss… the Husband of the Year who beat his wife to death with his winner's trophy… and the transvestite water goddess who killed 200…

Drawing on the limitless resources of the *FT* archives, *The Fortean Times Book of Inept Crime* gathers hundreds of the most bizarrely incompetent and peculiar burglaries, break-ins and bank jobs ever recorded in one paperback book.

£4.99   ISBN 1 870870 808

This title is available from all good book stores, or by phoning our telephone order hotline:

☎ 01789 490215